Learn How To Draw

Animals

by Ms. Karen L. McQuary

Fonts used: Arial and **Arial Black** - The Monotype Corporation, Big Ham - OMEGA Font Labs

If you can make a line, then you can create a drawing.
Drawings are a bunch of connected lines made with a purpose.

There are many types of lines

There are straight lines

lines that curve,

bumpy lines,

pointy lines

and even lines that spiral and swirl!

Thick and thin, alone or
together, you will use all these lines and more to create
the shapes that make your animal drawings.

Can you draw these basic shapes?

Drawings are made from many basic shapes!

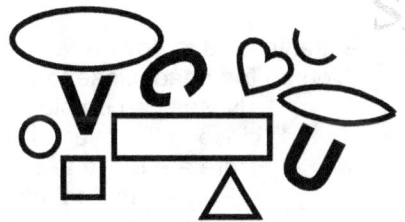

Many curves are created by making 'U' shapes.

Some shapes are made by making 'V' shapes.

There are circles,

half and partial circles,

Squares and hearts

There are 'football' shapes and

triangle shapes that make great 'pointy' ended shapes.

Ovals and rectangles make many great body shapes.

Look for shapes and IMAGINE those shapes as you draw.
(if you need to lightly sketch those shapes in- DO IT! That's why erasers were invented!)

How to Draw a Face

There are many ways to draw a face. Sometimes the eyes are high on the head, close together or far apart. Noses can be big or small, close to the eyes or far away. Here are just a few samples. Play around to find facial shapes that you like.

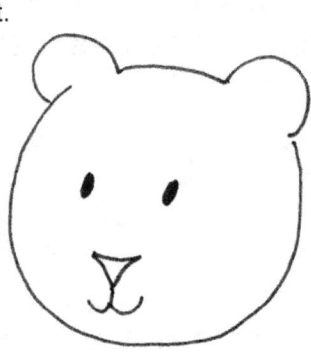

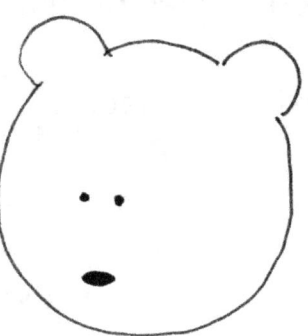

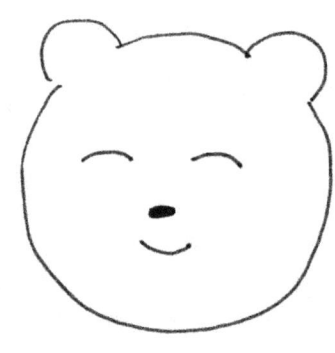

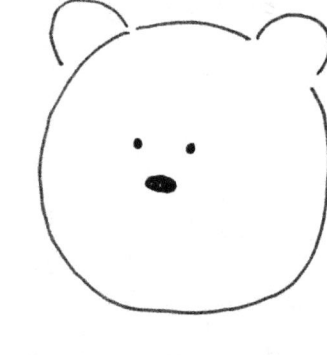

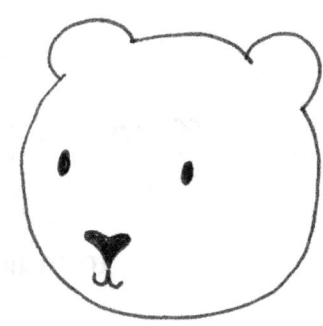

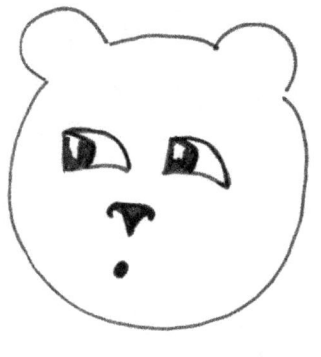

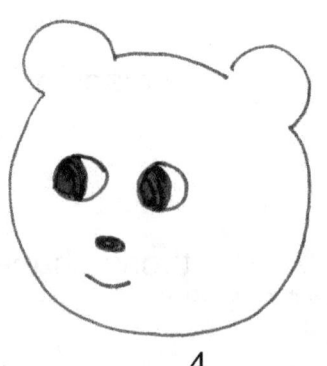

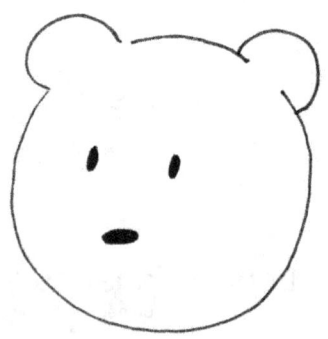

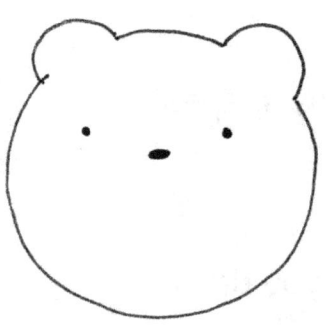

4

How to Draw an Alligator

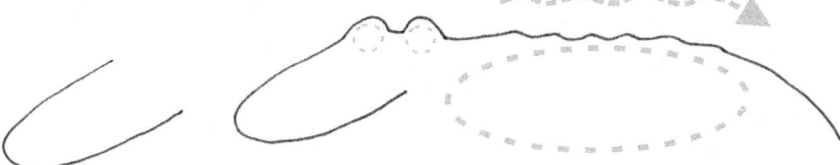

Draw a long 'U' shape.

Imagine 2 circle shapes and an oval. Draw around them to create the body. Draw a 'bumpy' line on the back to make the alligator's skin texture.

Imagine a circle that the tale will curve around.

Imagine 2 circles to create rounded legs and pointy toes. Connect them to the body by drawing a line for the stomach.

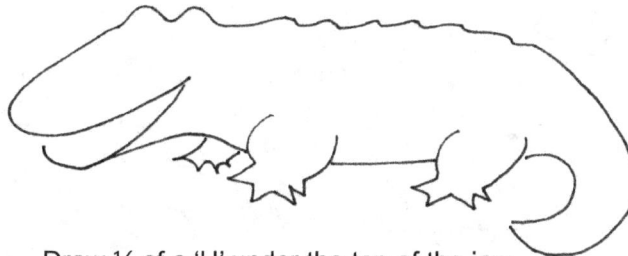

Draw ½ of a 'U' under the top of the jaw to create the mouth and connect it to the body by drawing the neck. Draw the other front foot by making pointy toes.

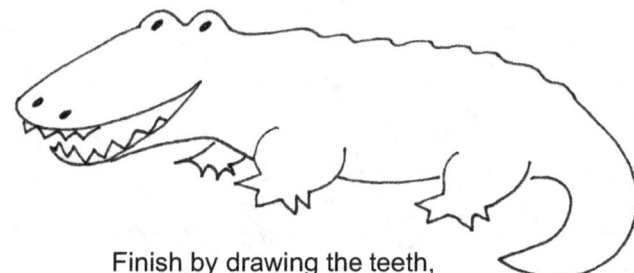

Finish by drawing the teeth, eyes and nostrils.

How to Draw a **Bear**

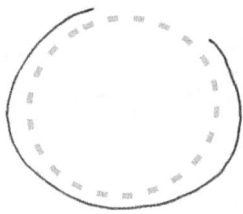

Draw a partial circle.

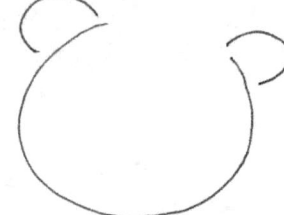

Add 2 half circles to create ears.

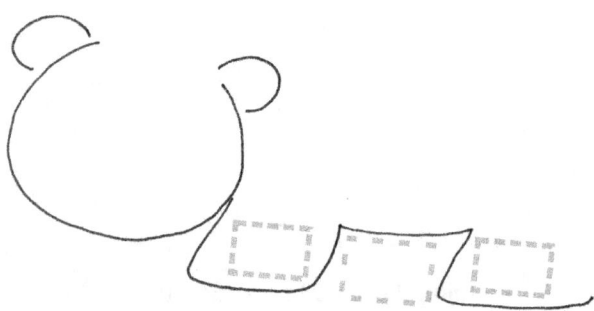

Imagine 3 rectangle shapes and draw around
them to create 2 wide legs and the space between.

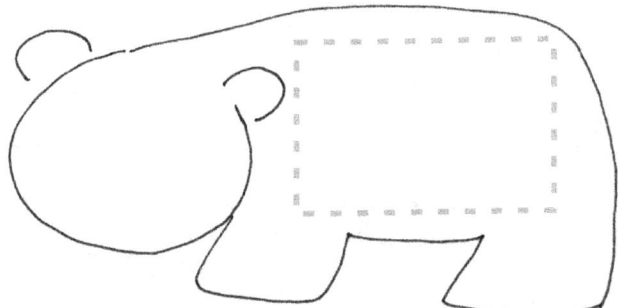

Imagine another large rectangle and
draw around it to connect
the back foot to the head.

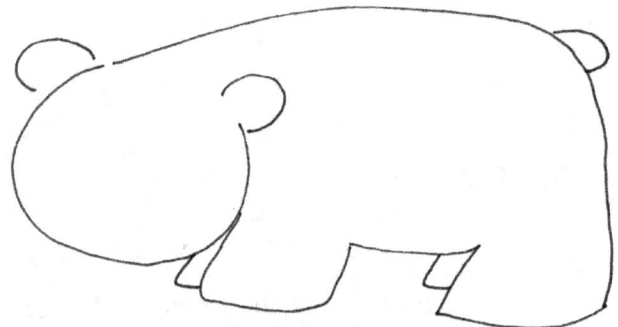

Draw the other two legs and a 'U' shaped tail.

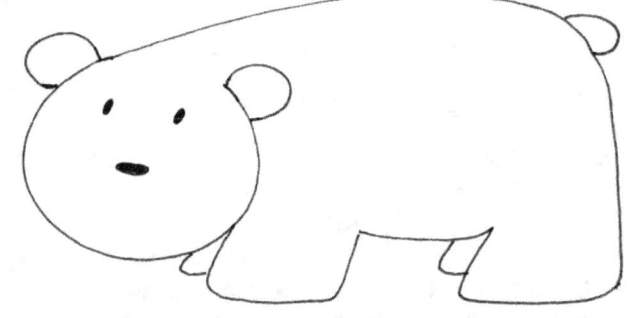

Finish by drawing a face.

6

How to Draw a Bunny

Imagine an oval.

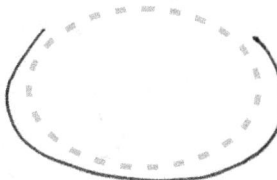

Draw the bottom of the oval.

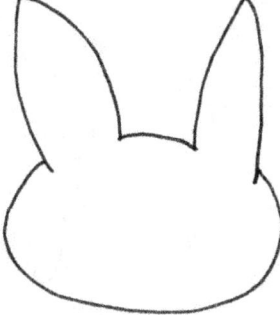

Add two long ears to the top.

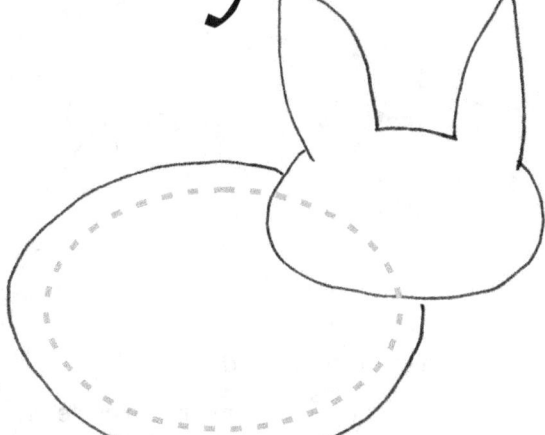

Imagine another large oval and draw around the oval for the body.

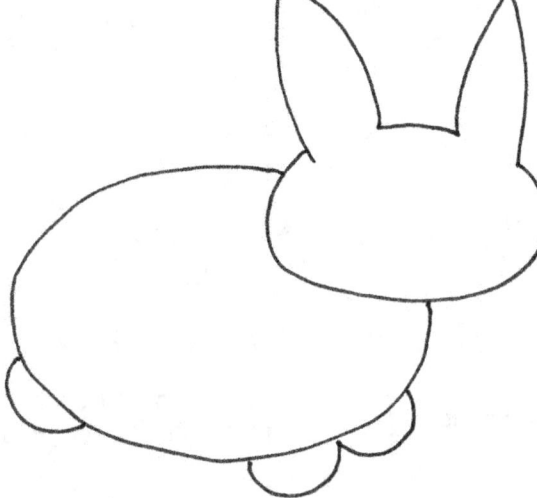

Draw 3 half circles for the feet.

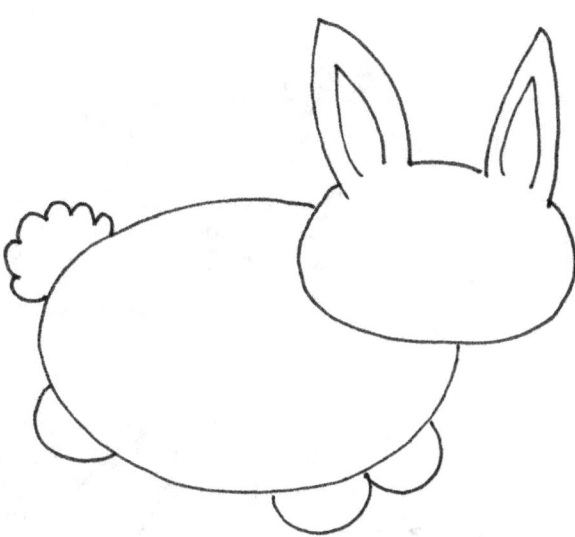

Add a puffy tail and draw another set of small ears inside the bigger ones.

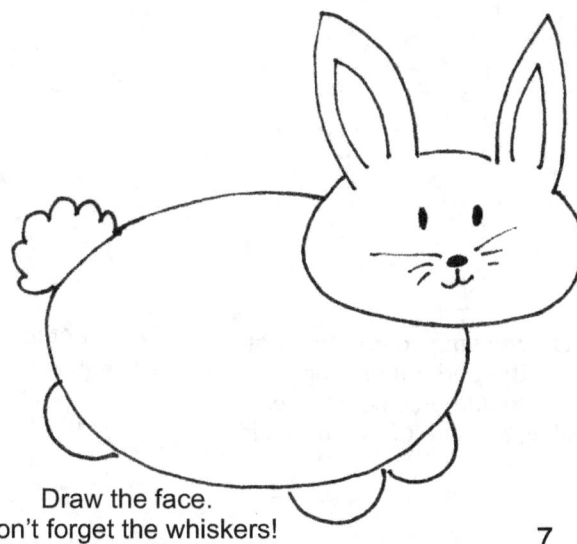

Draw the face.
Don't forget the whiskers!

7

How to Draw a Butterfly

#1 front view

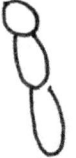

Draw a circle connected
to 2 ovals.

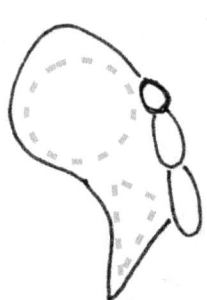

Imagine a circle and a triangle.
Draw around them to
create the first wing.

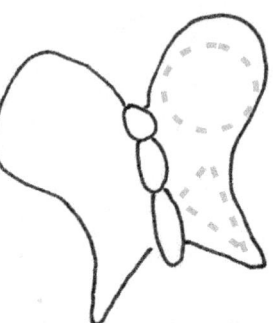

Draw the second wing
by creating the same shape
on the other side.

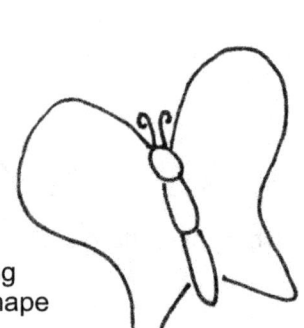

Add antennas.

#2 side view

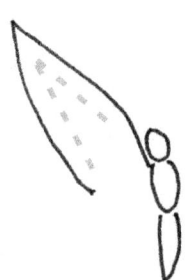

Draw a circle
connected
to 2 ovals.

Imagine a 'V' shape
and draw around it.

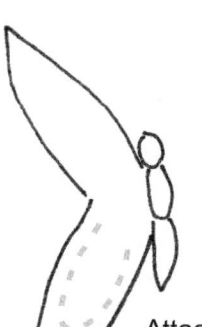

Attach it to a 'U' shape to
create the bottom wing.

Imagine a 'V' shape next to the tip
of the top wing. Leaving that space
open, draw the 2nd top wing using
the same shape as the 1st wing.
Connect the line to the
center of the head.

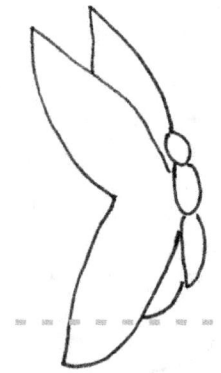

Draw a small curve to create
the 2nd bottom wing.
It should only come down
half the length of the front wing.

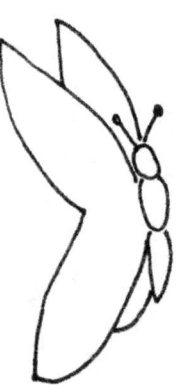

Draw antennas- one on
each side of the
line that creates
the back top wing.

8

How to Draw a 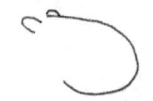 Camel

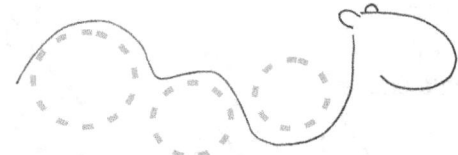

Draw a 'U' shape.

Add 2 small 'U' shapes
to create the ears.

Imagine 3 circles and draw around them
to create the camel's humps.

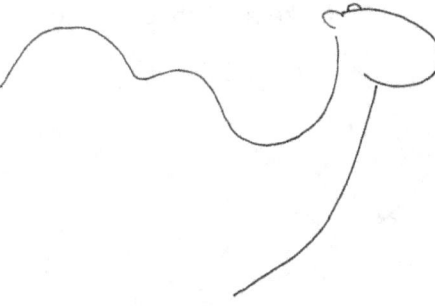

Draw a slight curve from the jaw
to create the throat and chest.

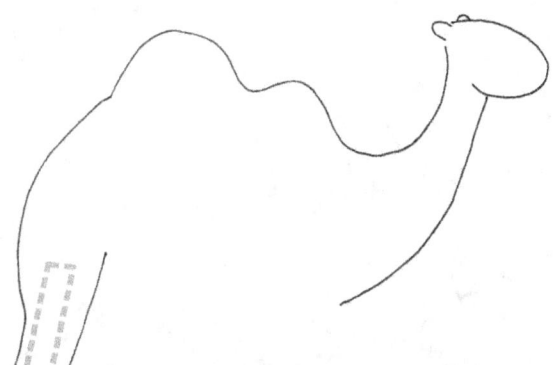

Draw a curve to create the back leg.
Imagine there are 2 rectangles
stacked on top of each other.
Notice the angles of each
part of the leg.

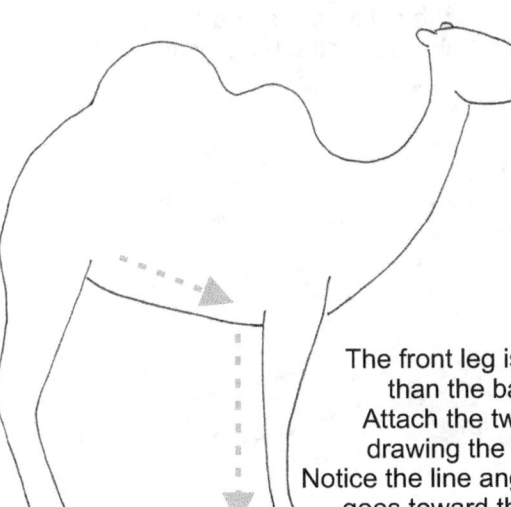

The front leg is straighter
than the back leg.
Attach the two legs by
drawing the stomach.
Notice the line angles down as it
goes toward the front leg.

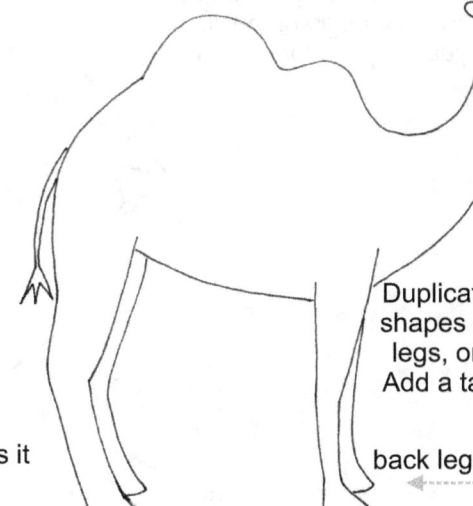

Duplicate the same
shapes for the back
legs, only shorter.
Add a tail and face.

back leg ends here

How to Draw a Cardinal

Draw a triangle shape.

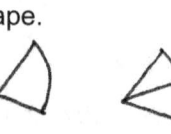

Split it in half.

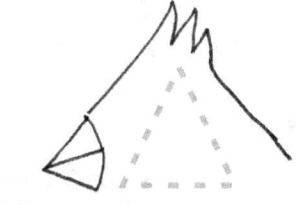

Extend the top side of the triangle and create 'pointy' feathers by making small triangles. (see the new triangle?)

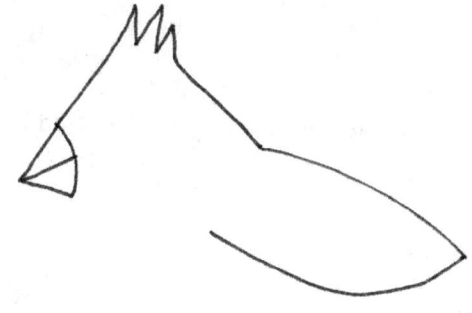

Make a 'U' shaped wing.

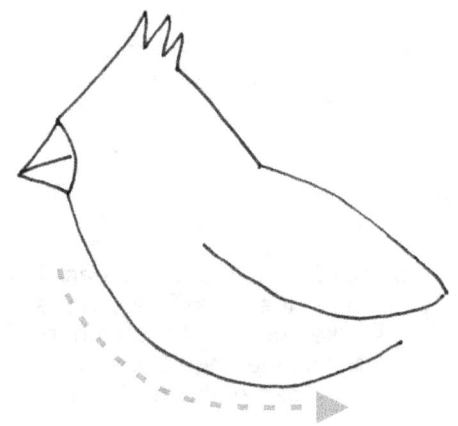

Starting at the base of the beak, make a large open curve towards the tip of the wing (leave space for the tail).

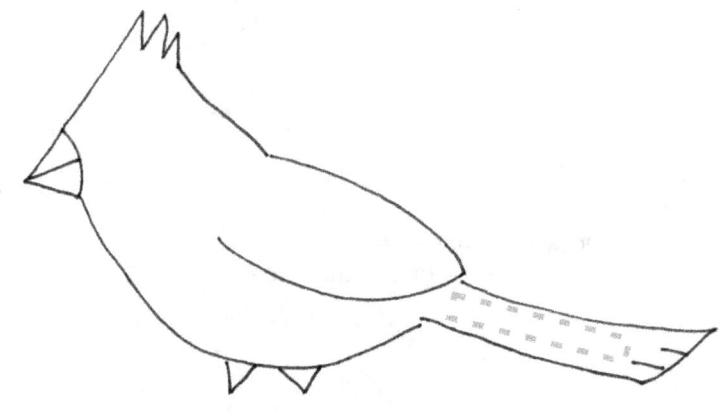

Make a long thin rectangle for the tail feathers and add 2 'V' shapes for the base of the legs.

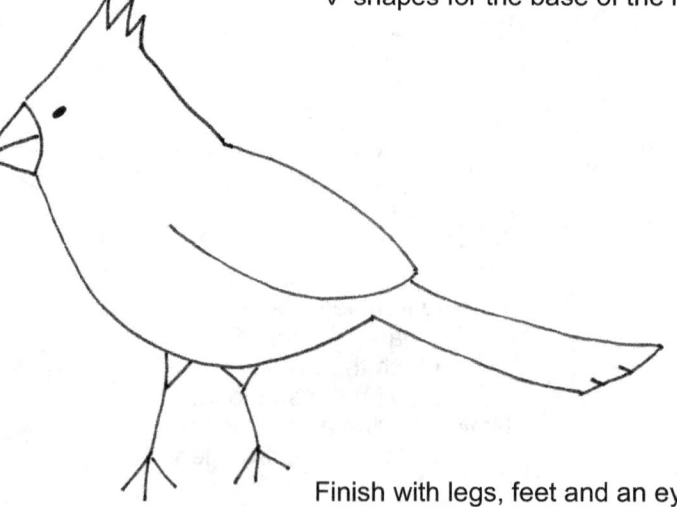

Finish with legs, feet and an eye.

10

How to Draw a Pudgy Cat

Imagine a circle.
Draw pointy fur around
the bottom half of the circle.

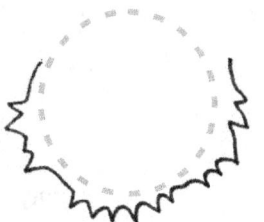

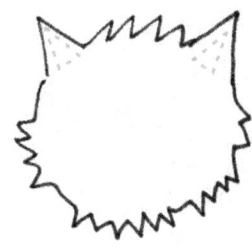

Draw two ears and pointy fur
between the two.
The ears are both triangle shaped.

Imagine an oval.
Starting
half way up
the head,
draw pointy fur
around the oval.
Leave open
spaces for the legs.

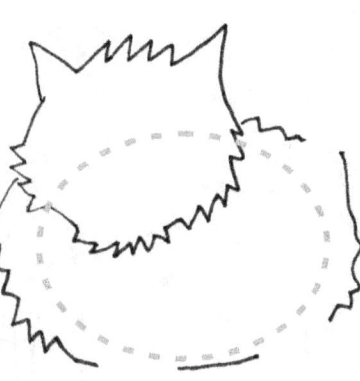

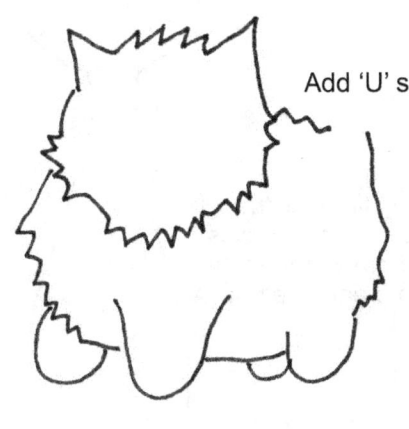

Add 'U' shaped legs.

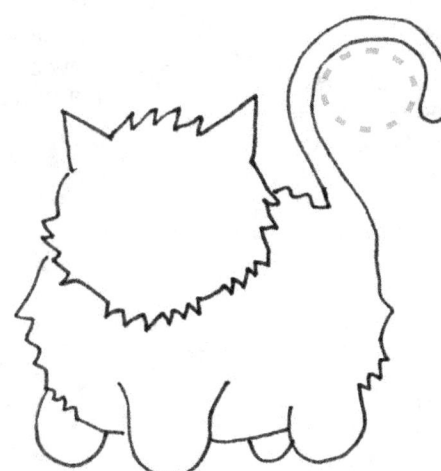

Imagine a circle and
create a curvy tail around it.

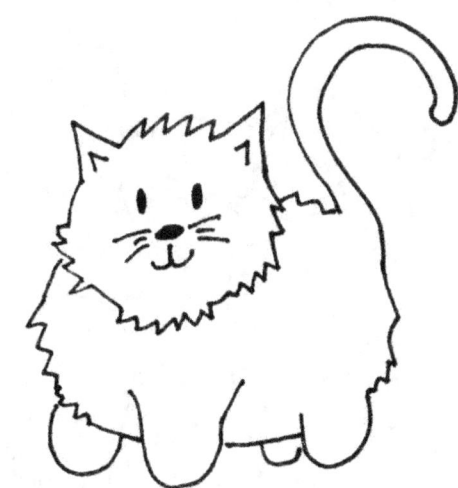

Add a face and small triangles inside the ears.

11

How to Draw a Skinny Kitty

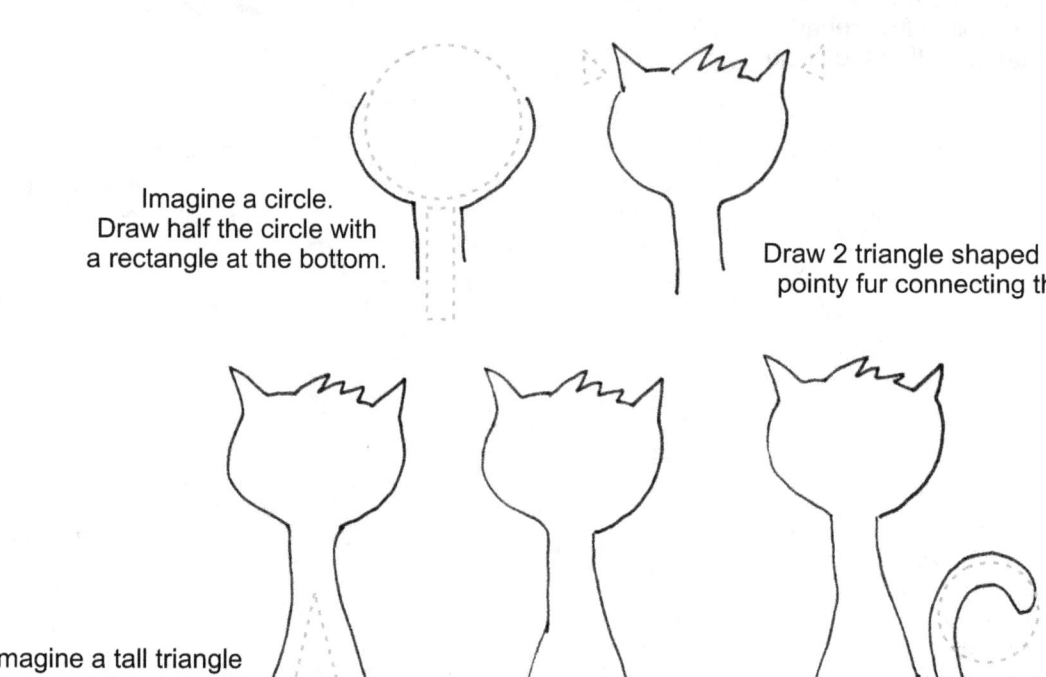

Imagine a circle.
Draw half the circle with
a rectangle at the bottom.

Draw 2 triangle shaped ears and
pointy fur connecting the ears.

Imagine a tall triangle
on top of 2 circles
and draw around them
to create the body.

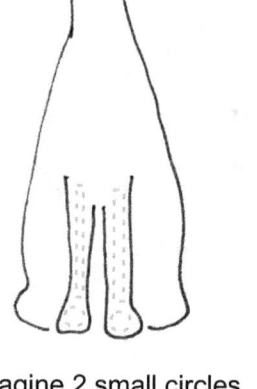

Imagine 2 small circles
topped by 2 long rectangles
to create the front legs.

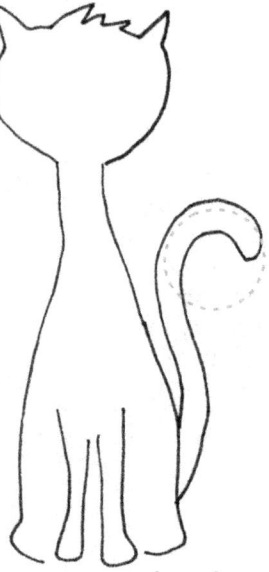

Imagine a circle.
Draw a long curve
tail around the circle.

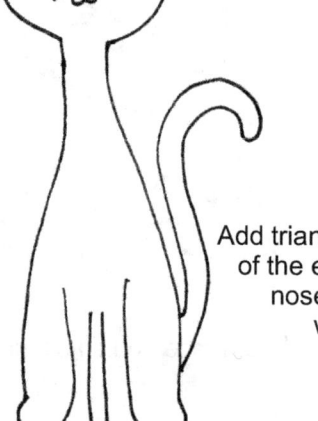

Add triangles to the inside
of the ears. Add eyes,
nose, mouth and
whiskers.

12

How to Draw a Chipmunk

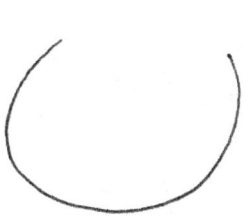

Draw a partial circle.

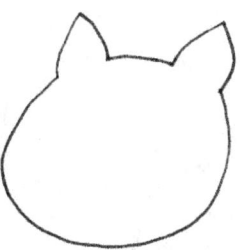

Add 2 'V' shapes to make the ears.

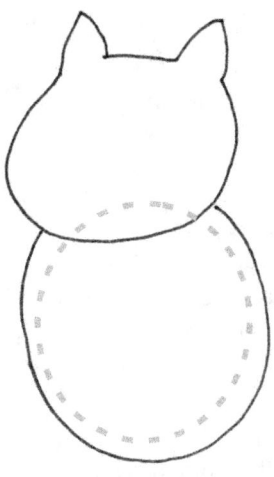

Imagine a circle and draw around it to form the body.

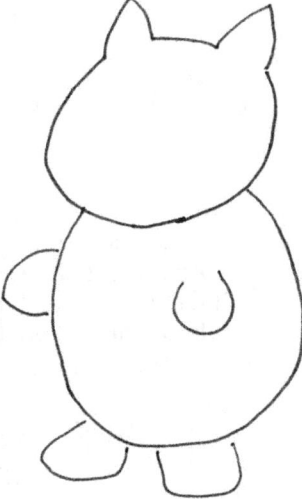

Draw 4 'U' shapes to create the hands and feet.

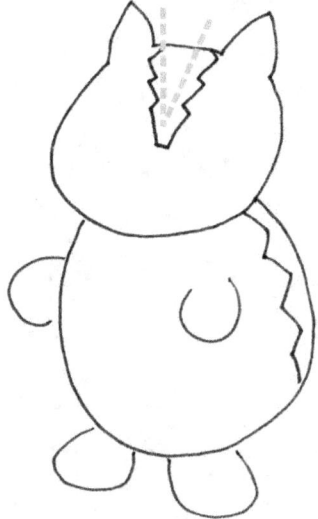

Following a 'v' shape, draw a 'pointy' stripe between the ears and half way down the face. Draw another 'pointy' stripe down the curve of the back.

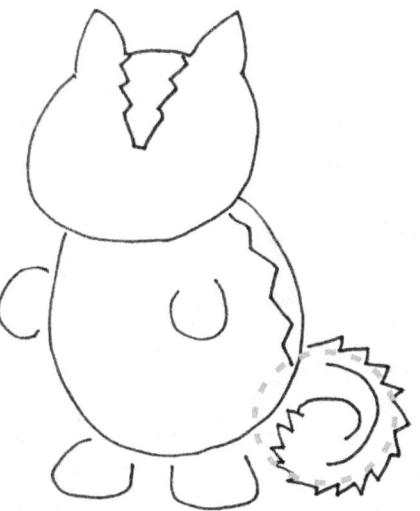

Imagine a circle and draw a 'pointy' spiral line around it to create a fuzzy tail.

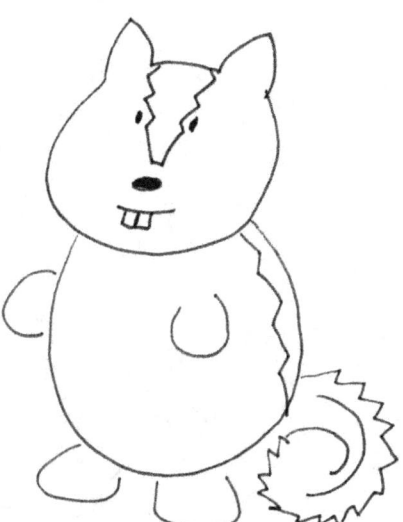

Finish with eyes, a nose and rectangle shaped teeth.

13

How to Draw a Coyote

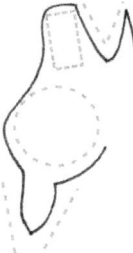

Imagine a circle and draw around it.
Add a 'V' shape for the ear.
The snout is a rectangle and the
mouth opening is another 'V' shape.

Starting at the chin, draw a
curved line down and
back up to chest level
creating a rectangle shape.

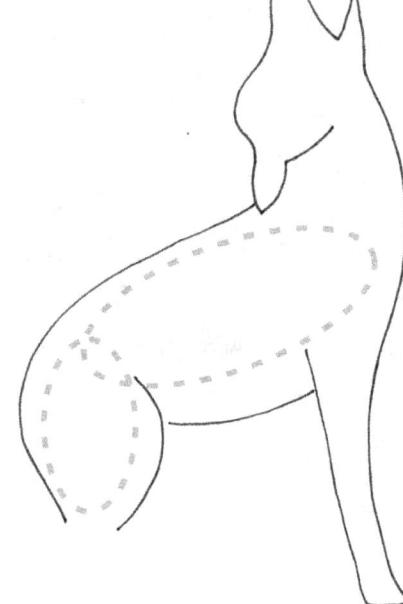

Imagine two ovals for the body and
leg. Draw around them to create
the body and back leg.

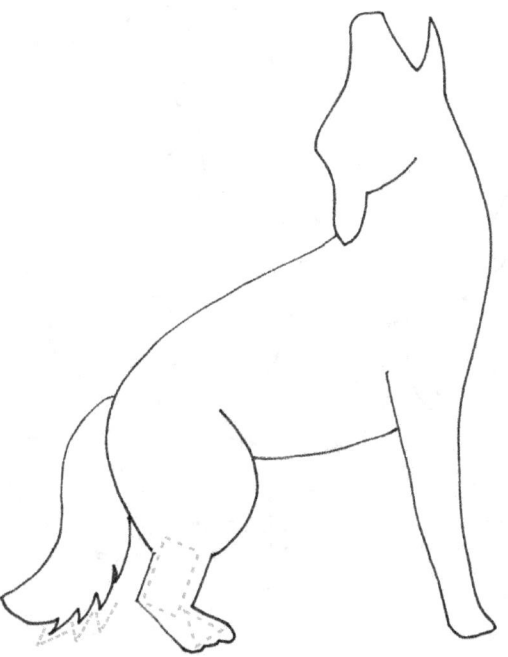

Imagine a rectangle and triangle for the foot.
Draw a bushy tail by using 'V' shapes to
make fur.

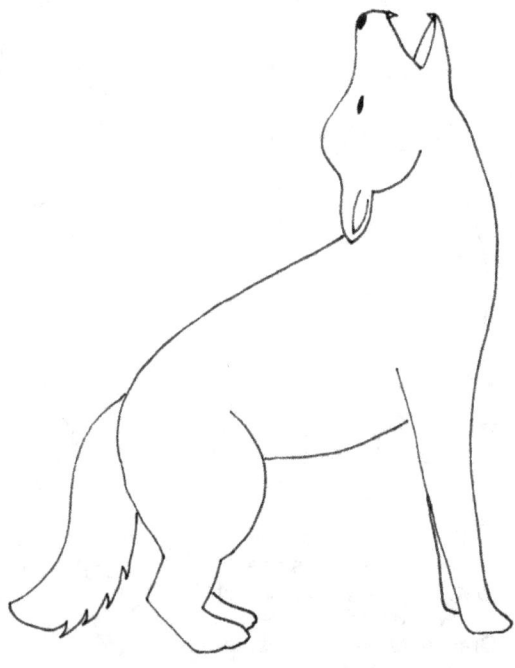

Finish with the feet, eye, nose, ear,
inside of the mouth and teeth.

14

How to Draw a Deer

Draw a 'U' shape for the head.

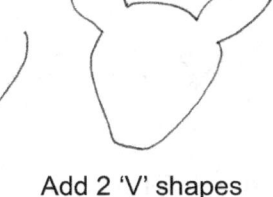

Add 2 'V' shapes for the ears and connect the top of the head.

From the center of the chin draw a straight line down.

Imagine the rectangle shapes and an oval. Draw around them to create the legs.

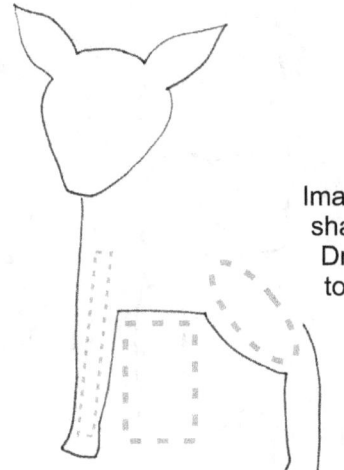

Imagine the oval shape to create the body. Draw a tail with pointy fur and connect the back to the head.

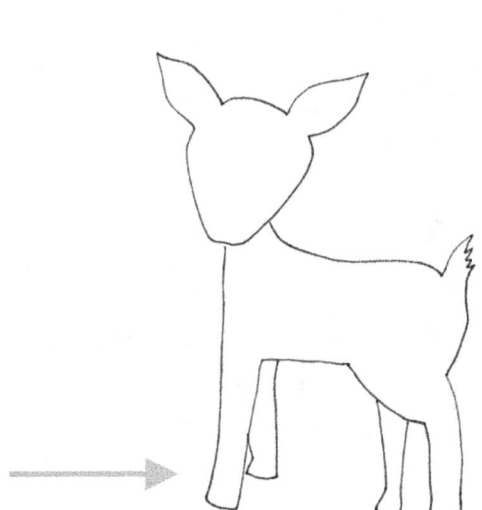

Draw the legs on the other side of the deer. Make sure the legs are drawn shorter.

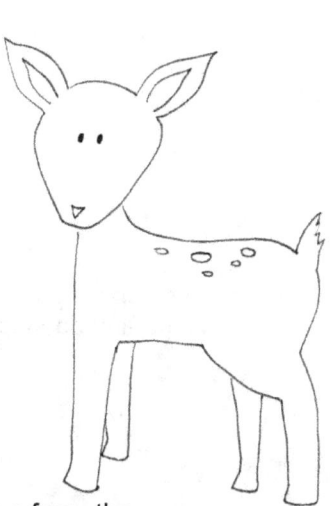

Finish with a face, the inner ears and spots.

15

Karen McQuary © 2010

How to Draw a
Boxer Dog

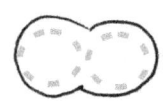
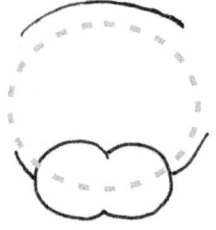
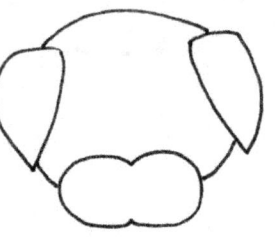
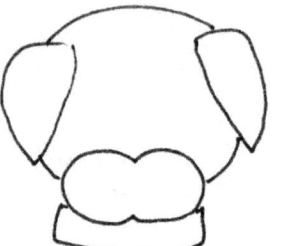

Imagine 2 circles.
Draw around t
create the snout.

Imagine a circle above.
Draw the top and
sides of the head.

Fill in the ears.
They look like
upside down teardrops.

Add the collar.

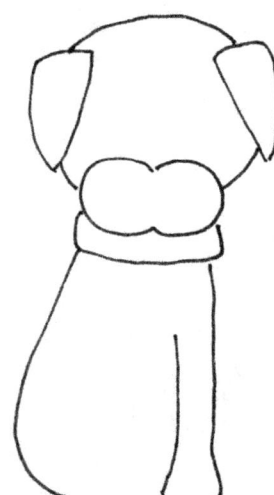
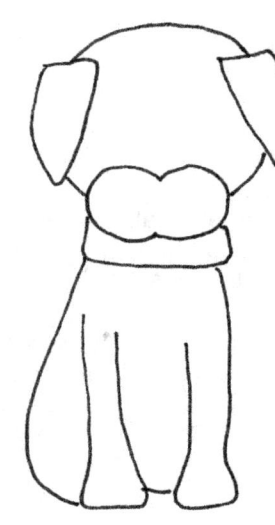
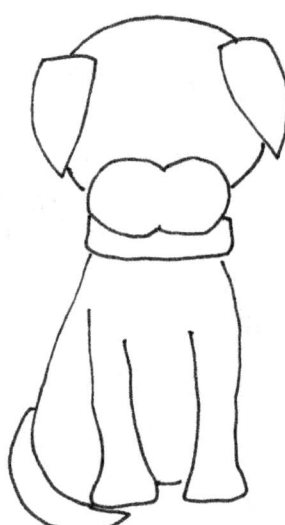

Add the side and one leg.

Match the other leg in height.

Draw a tail.

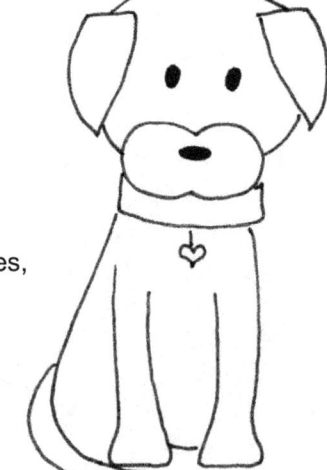

Finish by drawing the eyes,
nose and dog tag.

How to Draw a Maltese Dog

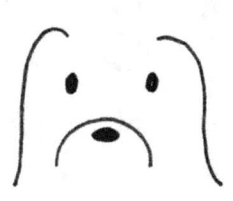

Draw eyes and nose. Create curved lines around the face.

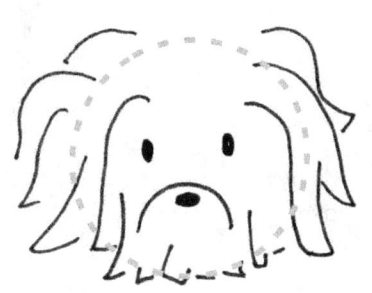

Imagine a circle. Continue curves around the circle.

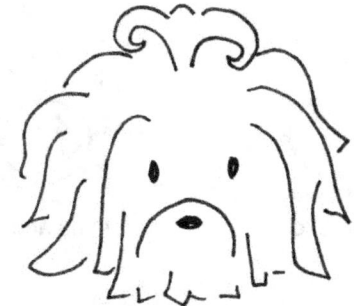

Draw a ponytail on the top of the head.

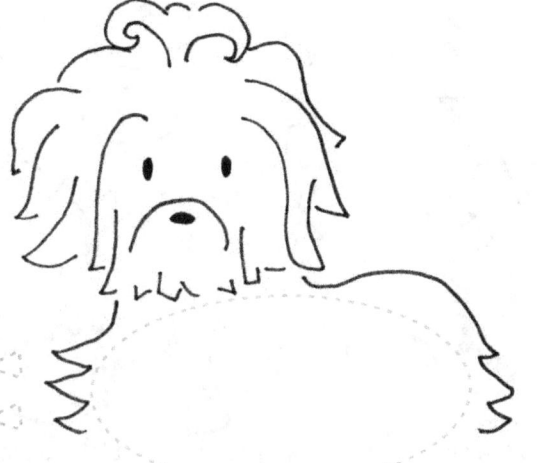

Imagine an oval and draw pointy hair by making sideways triangle shapes.

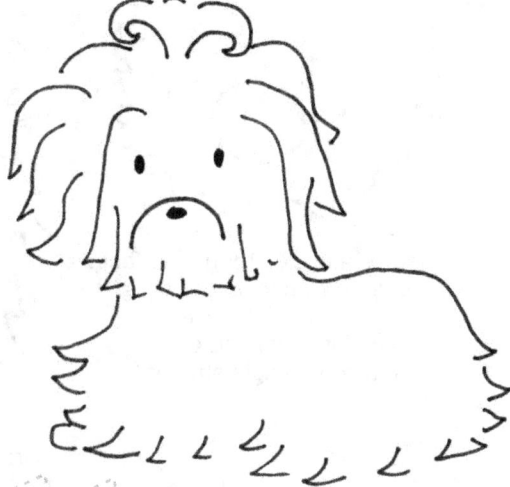

Continue to draw sideways triangle shapes along the bottom.

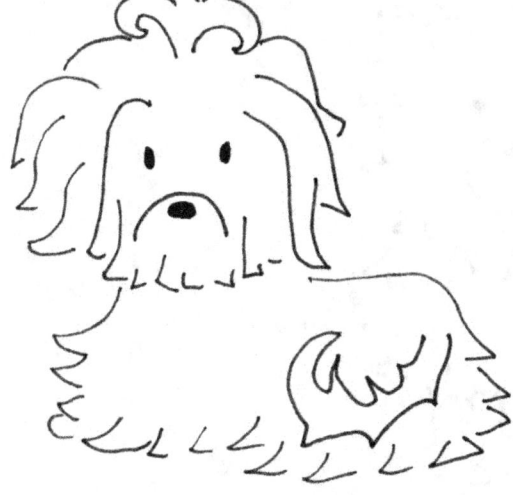

Draw a pointy fur tail.

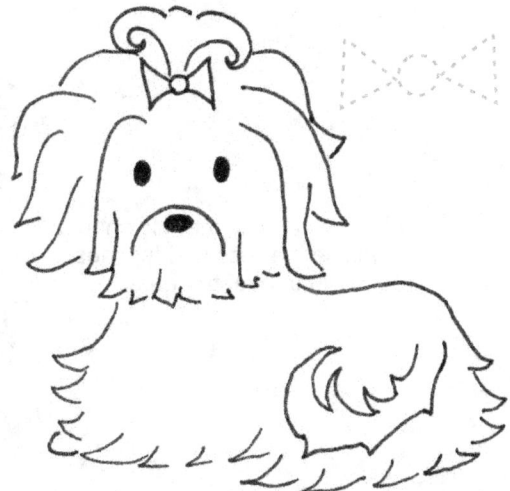

Finish with a bow at the bottom of the ponytail by drawing a circle and two triangles.

17

How to Draw a Pomeranian Dog

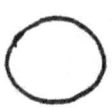

Draw a circle.

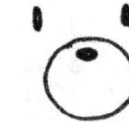

Add eyes and a nose.

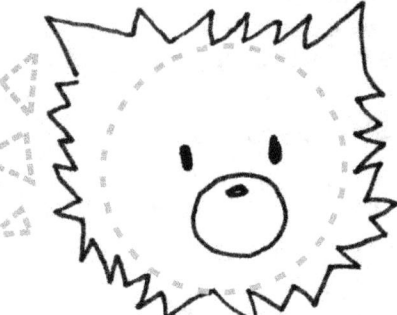

Imagine a circle around the face.
Create pointy fur and ears
around the circle.
Fur is created by
making triangle shapes.

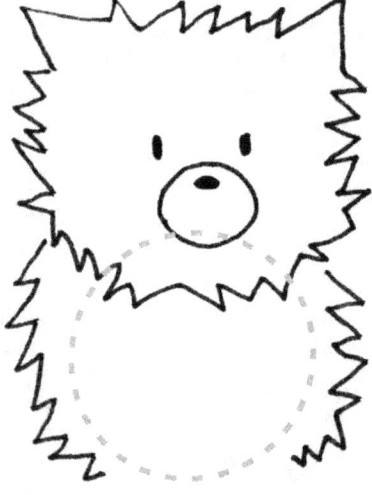

Imagine a second circle.
Create pointy fur around the side
but leave space for the legs.

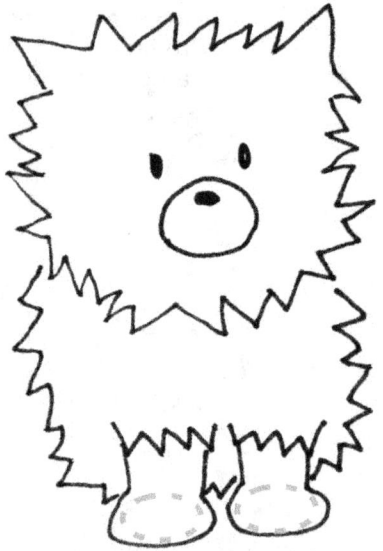

Imagine 2 ovals and draw
around them to create the
front legs. Add pointy fur
at the top of the legs.

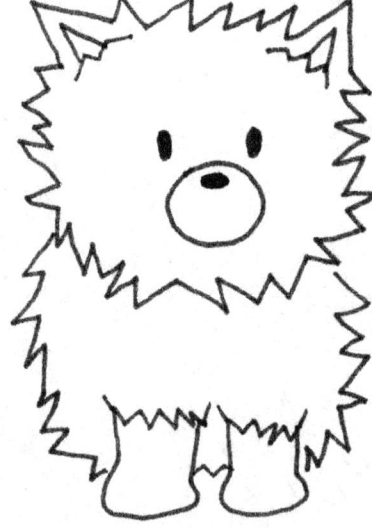

Finish by adding triangle shapes
inside the ears and fur lines
in front of the ears.

How to Draw a Puppy

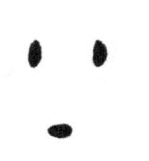

Draw eyes and a nose.

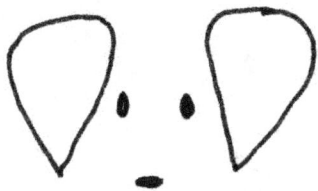

Add ears by drawing 2 upside down teardrop shapes.

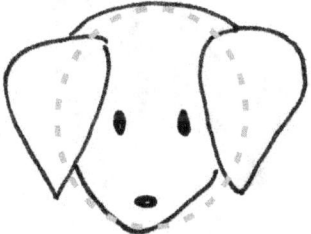

Imagine an oval shape and draw the head a little smaller than the ears.

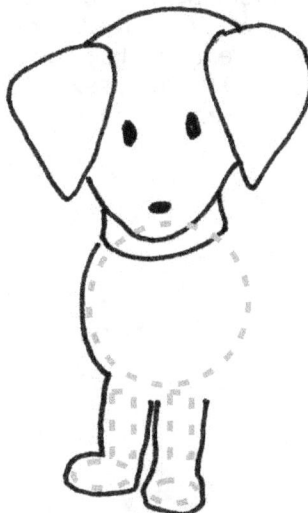

Add a collar. Imagine a circle, 2 rectangles and 2 ovals. Draw around them to create the body and front legs.

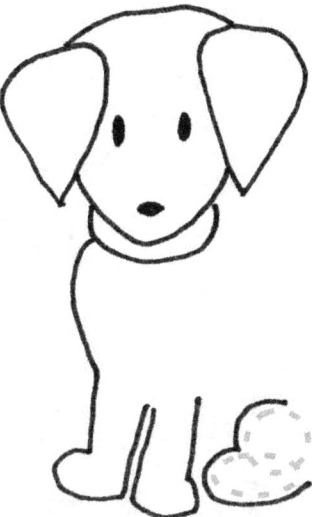

Imagine a circle and oval. Draw around them to create a back leg.

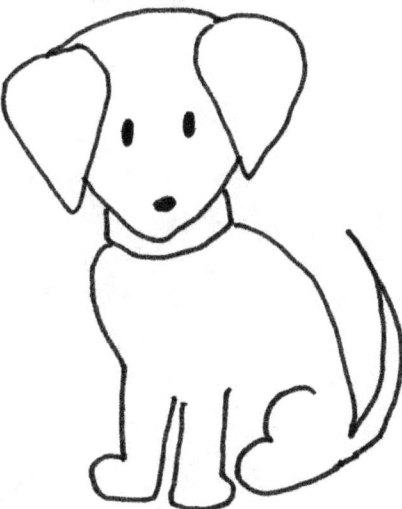

Add a tail and attach a curve along the back to the head.

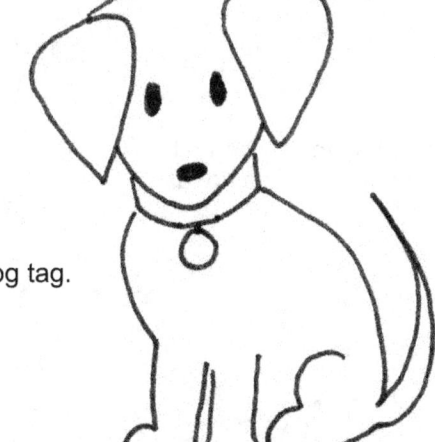

Add a dog tag.

19

How to Draw a Dolphin

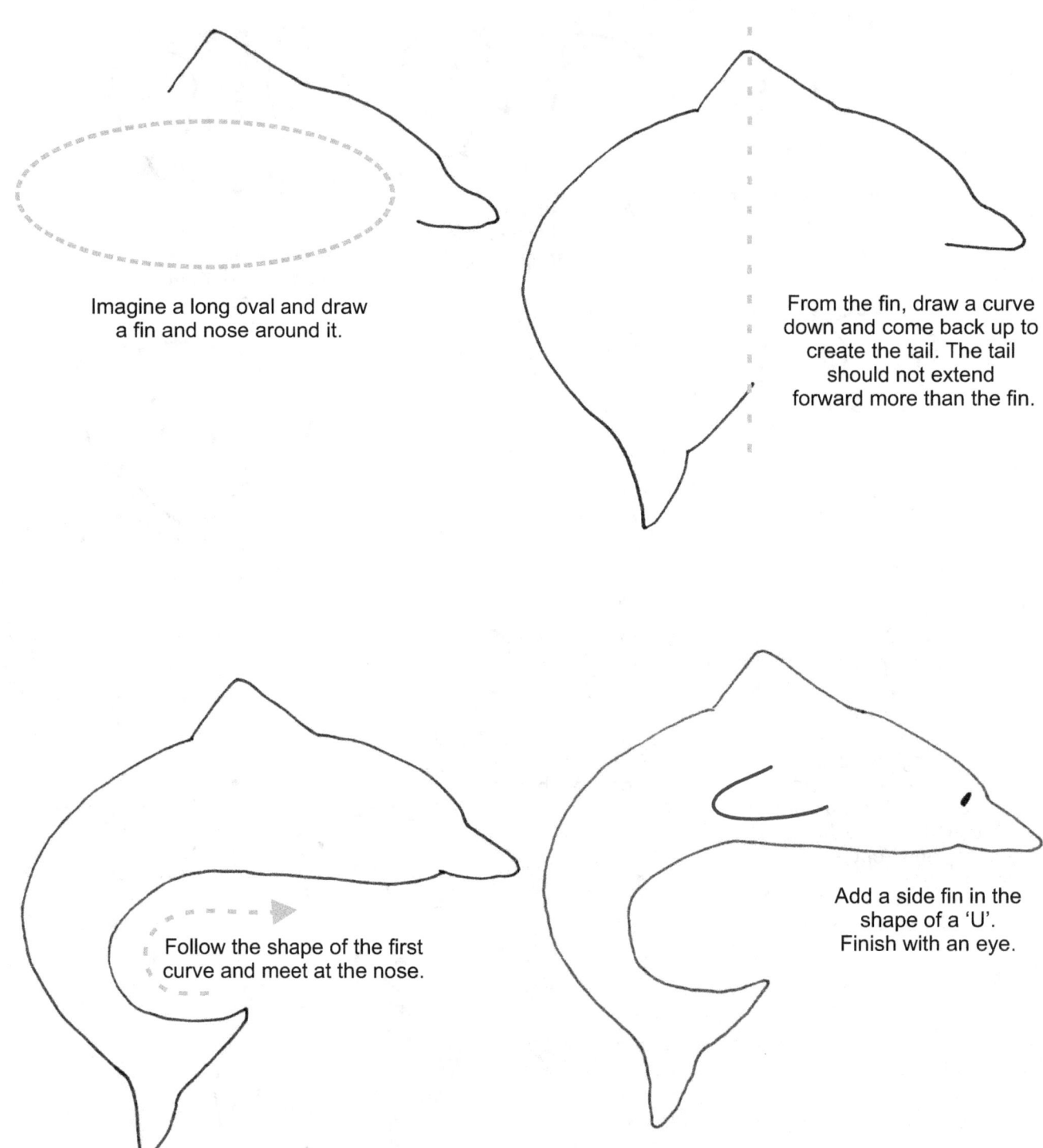

Imagine a long oval and draw a fin and nose around it.

From the fin, draw a curve down and come back up to create the tail. The tail should not extend forward more than the fin.

Follow the shape of the first curve and meet at the nose.

Add a side fin in the shape of a 'U'. Finish with an eye.

How to Draw a Dragonfly

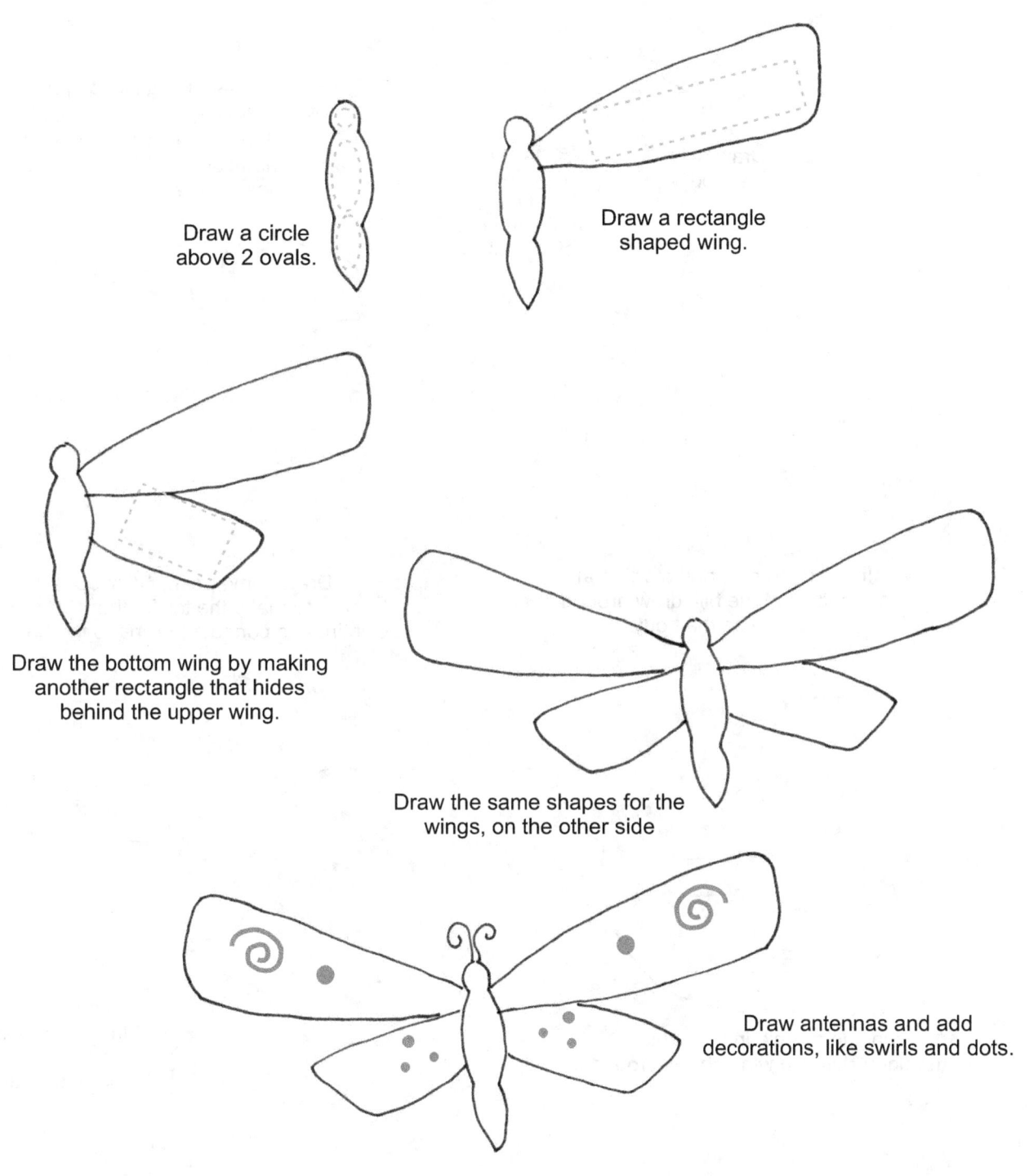

Draw a circle above 2 ovals.

Draw a rectangle shaped wing.

Draw the bottom wing by making another rectangle that hides behind the upper wing.

Draw the same shapes for the wings, on the other side

Draw antennas and add decorations, like swirls and dots.

How to Draw a Duck

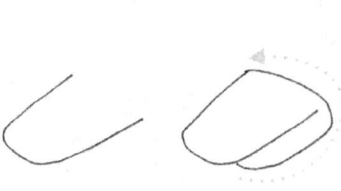

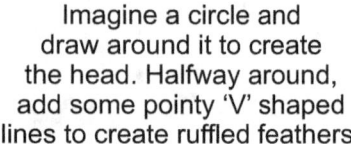

Draw a 'U' shape.

Draw a curve all the way around the 'U' to make the rest of the bill.

Imagine a circle and draw around it to create the head. Halfway around, add some pointy 'V' shaped lines to create ruffled feathers.

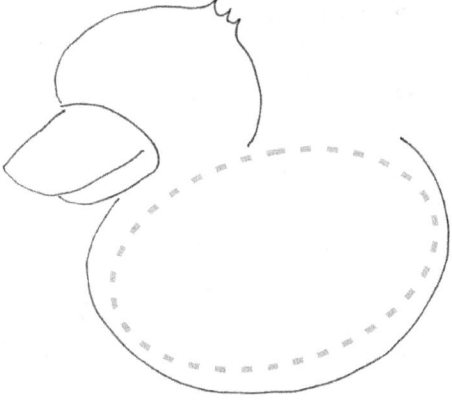

Imagine an oval and starting at the bottom of the bill, draw around it to create the body.

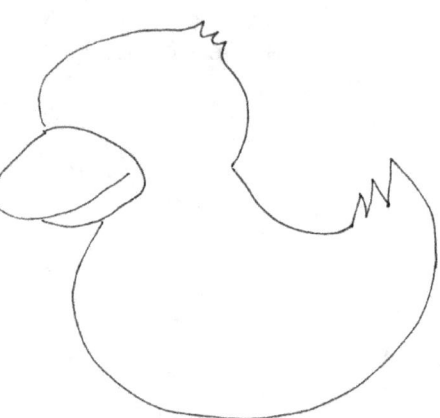

Draw some pointy 'V' shapes to make the tail feathers. Continue to connect the line to the head.

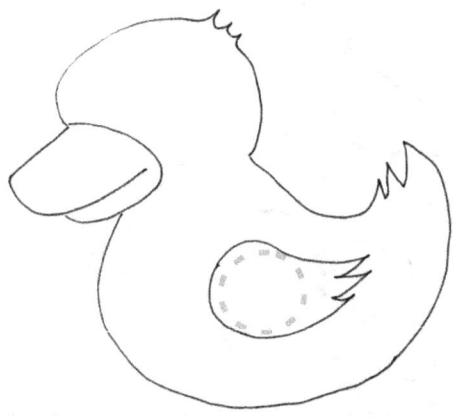

Imagine a circle in the center of the body. Draw a wing shape around it.

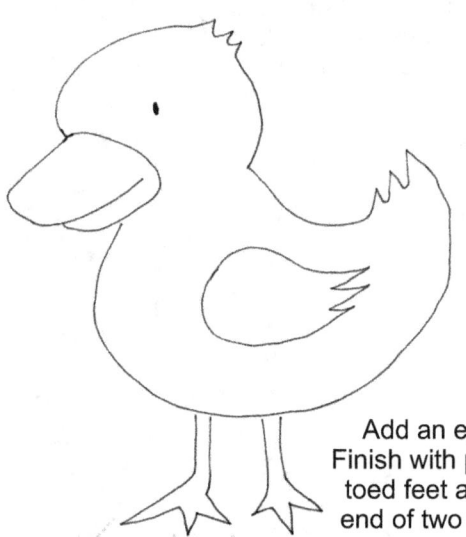

Add an eye. Finish with pointy toed feet at the end of two legs.

22

How to Draw an Elephant

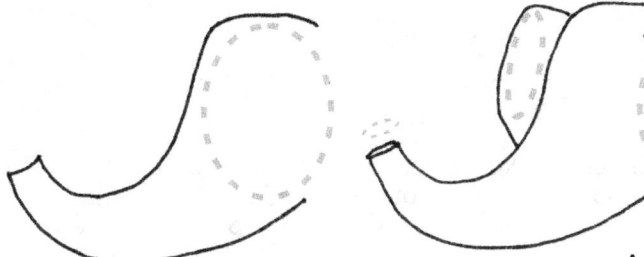

Imagine an oval and
draw a trunk around it.

Add ears and the end of the
trunk, which are all ovals.

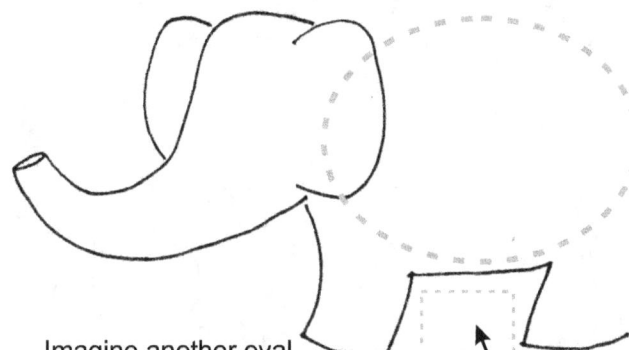

Imagine another oval.
Start from under the ear,
and add two legs.

See the square shape
between the two legs.

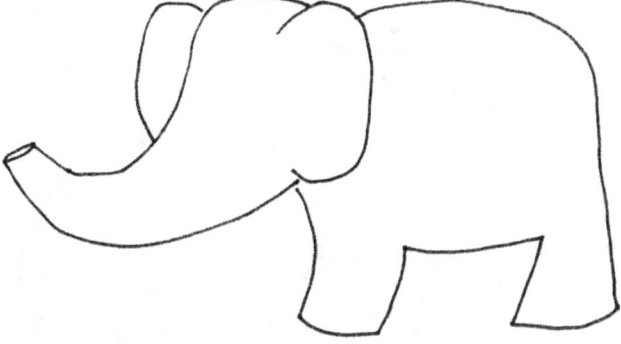

Draw a curved back and attach to the head.

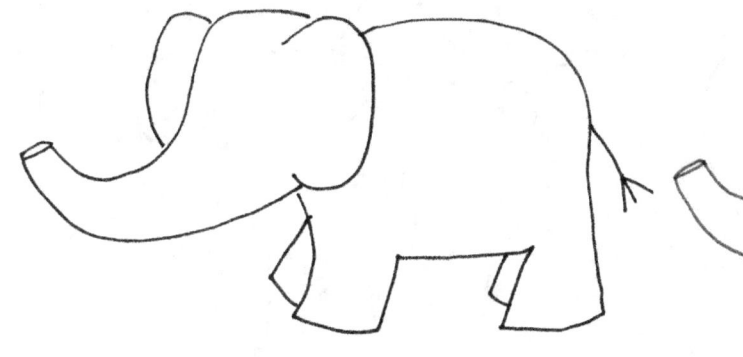

Draw a tail and 2 more legs.

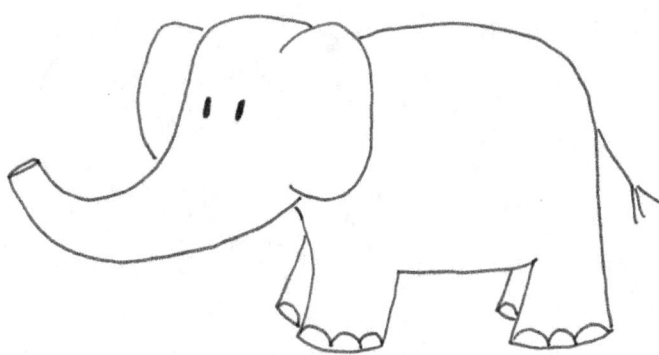

Add eyes and use half circles for toenails.

23

How to Draw a FOX

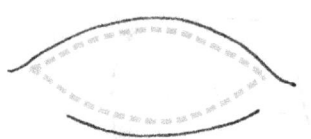

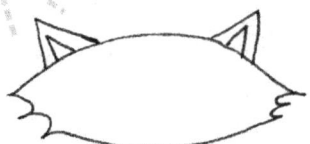

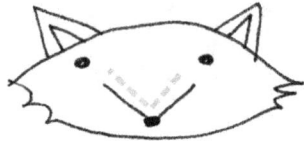

Draw a football shape with the ends left open.

Draw pointy fur at the ends of the football and add 2 ears by drawing 'V' shapes.

Draw a 'V' shape to make the snout and add eyes and a nose.

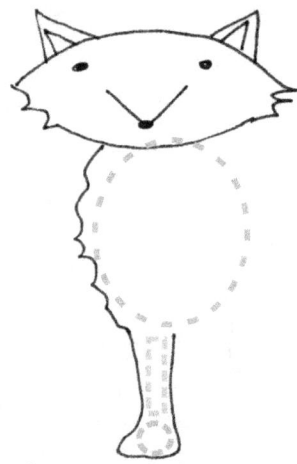

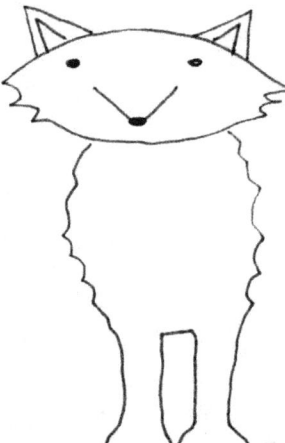

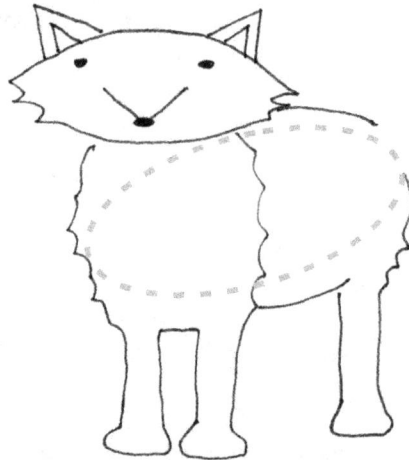

Imagine an oval shape on top of a rectangle, on top of a circle. Draw around them to create the chest and leg. Use small pointy marks for the fur on the chest.

Match the 2nd leg to the 1st.

Imagine an oval for the body and starting at the head draw around it, leaving a space for the tail. Match the back leg shape to the others.

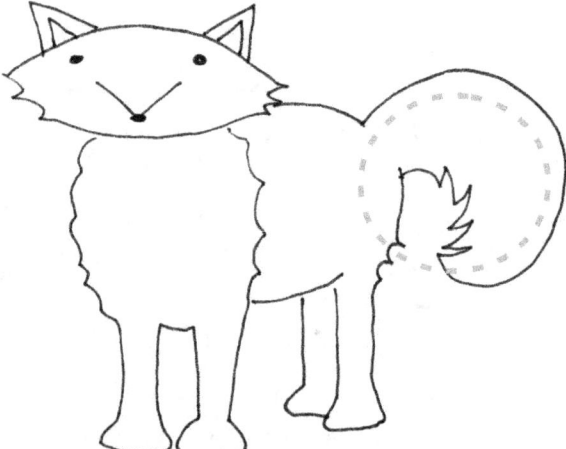

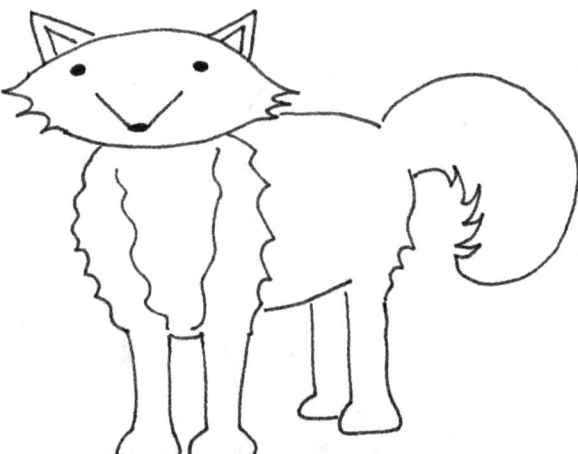

Imagine a circle and follow the curve for the tail. Make the underside of the tail with pointy edges for fur.

Finish with a squiggly line to create a stripe of fur on the chest.

24

How to Draw a Frog

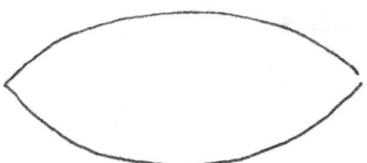

Draw a football shape.

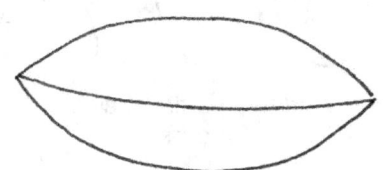

Draw a line cutting the football in half.

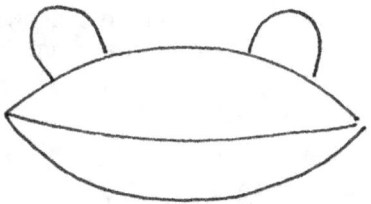

Add two upside down 'U' shapes for the eyes.

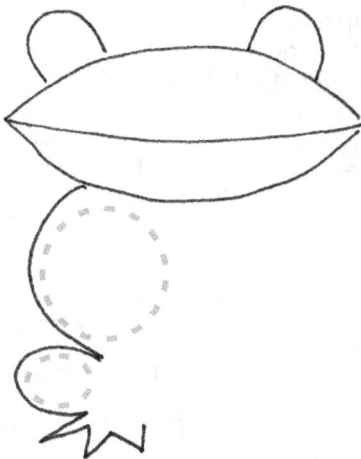

Imagine a circle and an oval. Draw around them to create the side and leg of the frog. The foot is pointy.

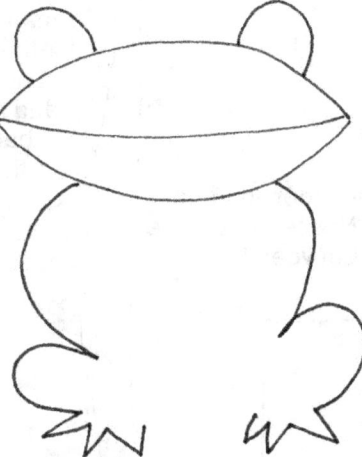

Match the other side.

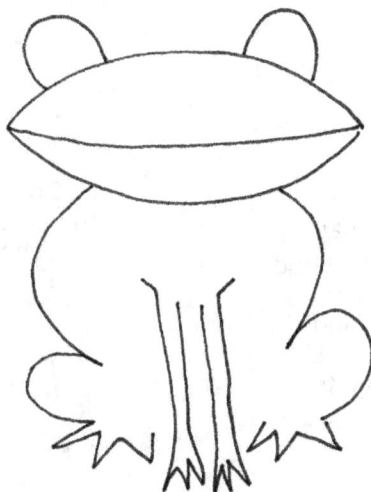

Add two long legs with pointy toes.

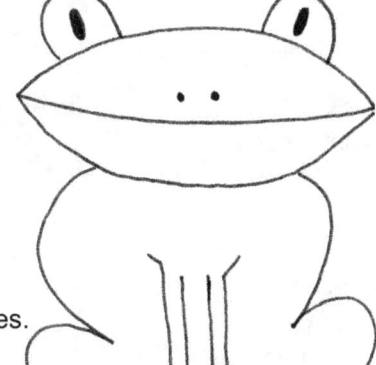

Finish the nose and eyes.

25

How to Draw a Giraffe

Imagine an oval and draw a 'U' shape around it.

Add two partial circles for ears.

Add antlers.

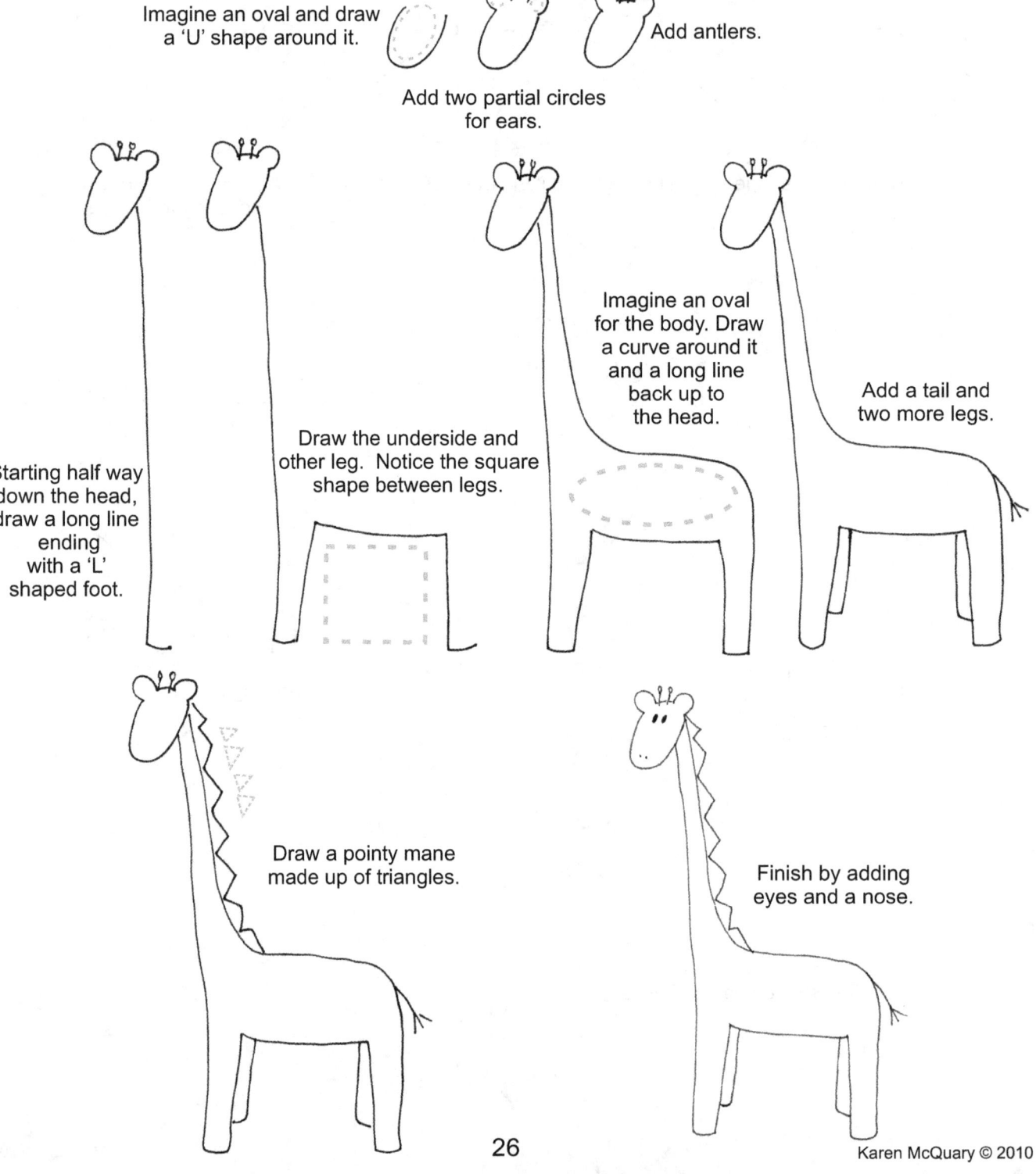

Starting half way down the head, draw a long line ending with a 'L' shaped foot.

Draw the underside and other leg. Notice the square shape between legs.

Imagine an oval for the body. Draw a curve around it and a long line back up to the head.

Add a tail and two more legs.

Draw a pointy mane made up of triangles.

Finish by adding eyes and a nose.

How to Draw a Hippo

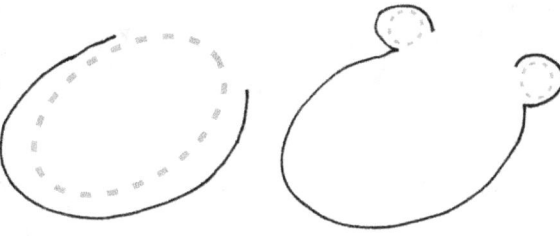

Imagine an oval and draw a 'U' shape around it.

Imagine 2 circles. Draw 'U' shapes around them to make the ears.

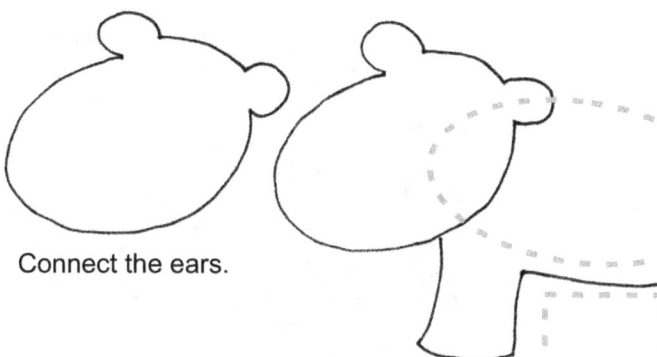

Connect the ears.

Imagine an oval and starting by the chin, create the front leg. Continue with the underside and draw around a square shape.

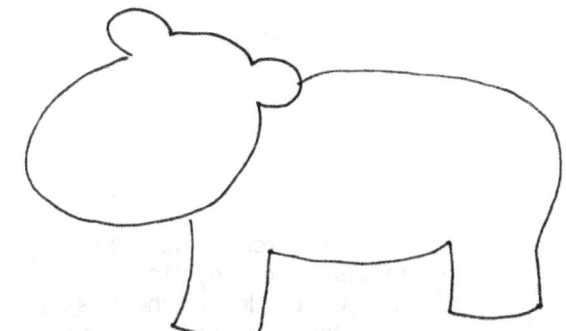

Continue the curve around the body oval and meet at the ear.

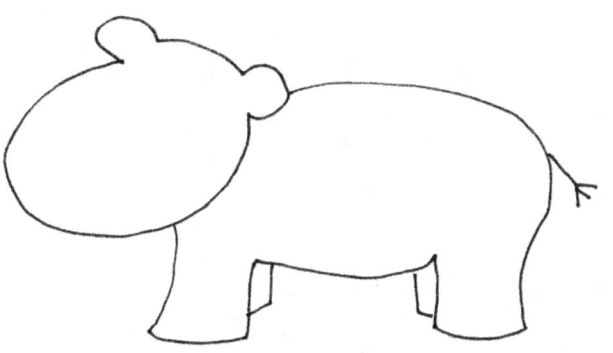

Add a tail and two more legs.

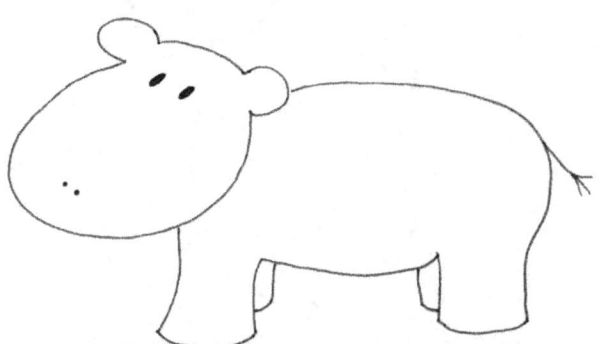

Finish by adding eyes and a nose.

How to Draw a Kangaroo

Draw a 'U' shape.

Add 2 'V' shapes to make ears.

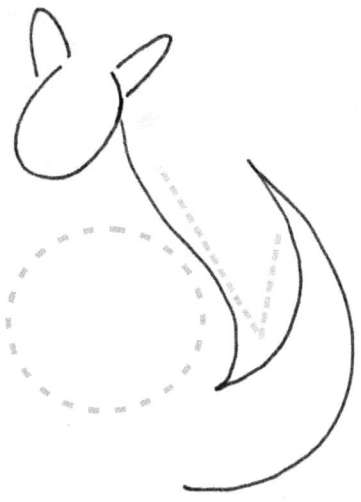

Imagine a circle to draw around to create the body. To get the curve of the tail, look at the 'V' shape located between the body and tail.

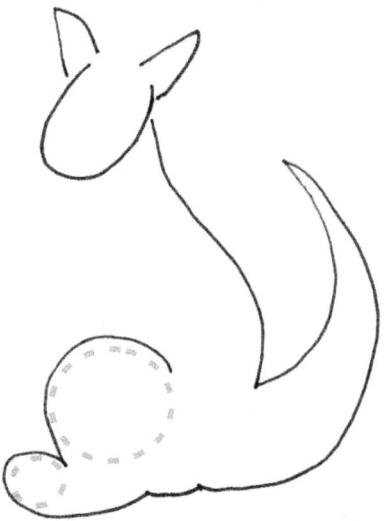

Imagine 2 circles and draw around them to create the leg and foot.

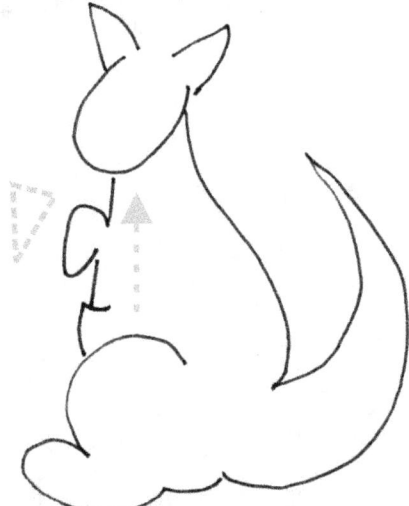

The front of the body follows a straight line. The hand is shaped like a triangle.

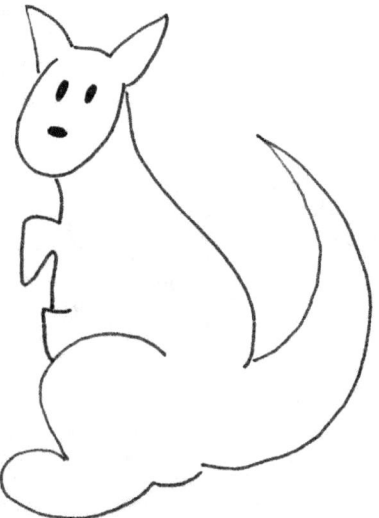

Finish by adding a face.

How to Draw a Koala Bear

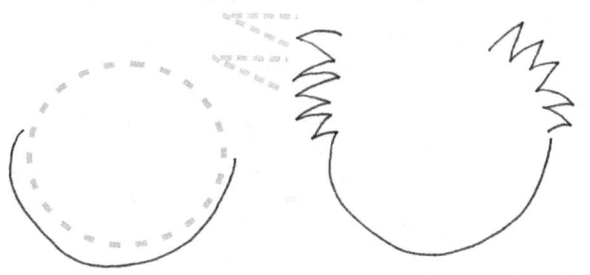

Draw a partial circle.
Add some pointy 'V' shapes to create hairy ears.

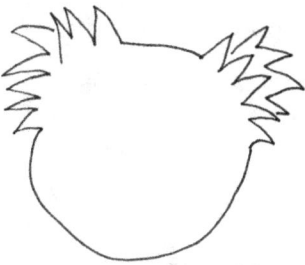

Add a 2nd layer of hair to the ears.

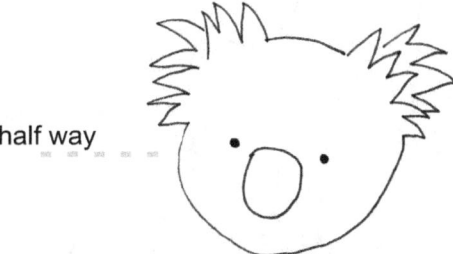

half way

Draw a wide oval nose. Nose should not be higher than ½ way up the face.

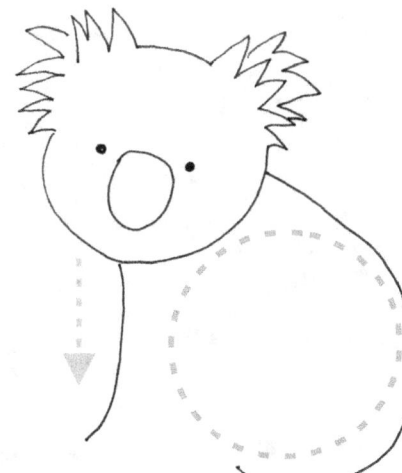

Imagine a large circle and draw the curve around it to create the back. The front leg is a slightly curved downstroke.

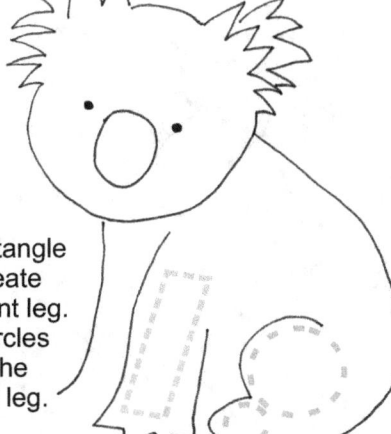

Imagine a rectangle shape to create the closest front leg. Imagine 2 circles to create the closest back leg.

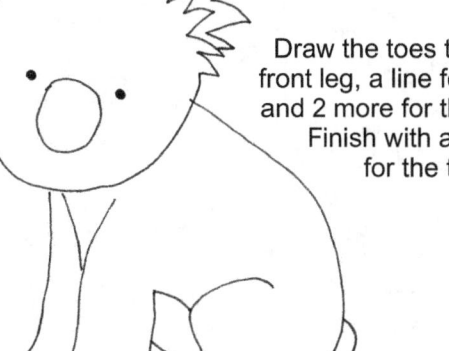

Draw the toes to the other front leg, a line for the chest, and 2 more for the stomach. Finish with a ½ circle for the tail.

How to Draw a Leopard

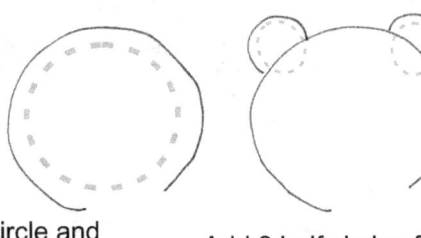

Imagine a circle and draw a partial circle around it to create the head.

Add 2 half circles for ears.

Starting at the circle opening, draw down to make a long 'L' shape to create the foot. Draw a bumpy line of toes.

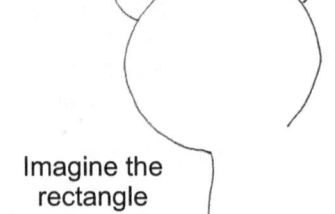

Imagine the rectangle shape and draw around it to create the stomach and back leg.

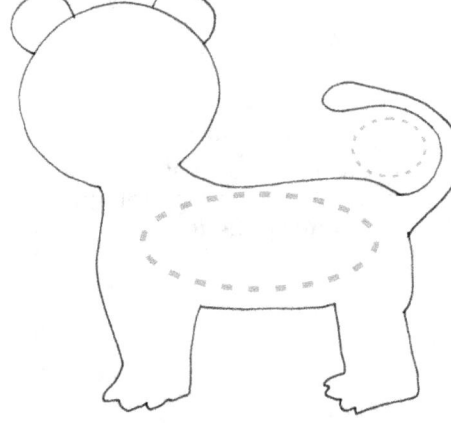

Imagine an oval shape for the body. When you draw around it, leave space for the tail. As the tail curves up, imagine a circle space between the tail and body.

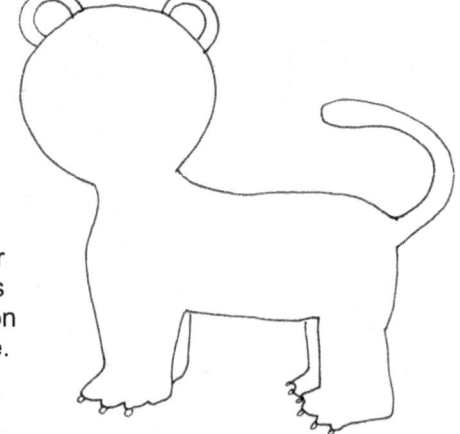

Add the inner ears, toenails and the legs on the other side.

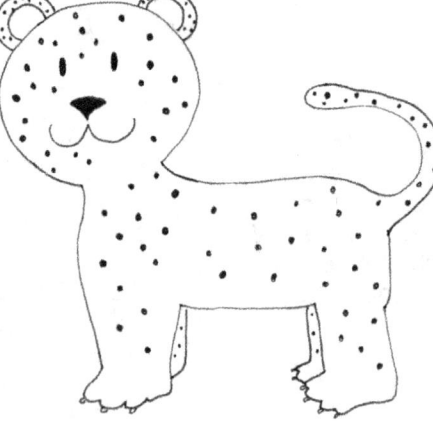

Finish with a face and lots of spots.

30

How to Draw a Lion

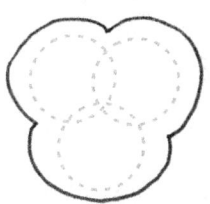

Imagine 3 overlapping circles. Draw around.

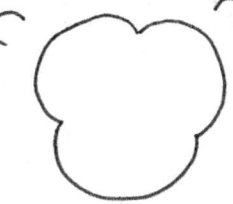

Add 2 half circles away from the face.

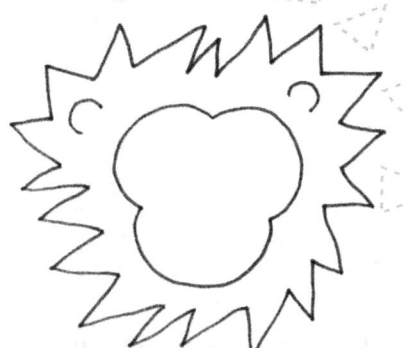

Draw the mane pointy by using triangle shapes.

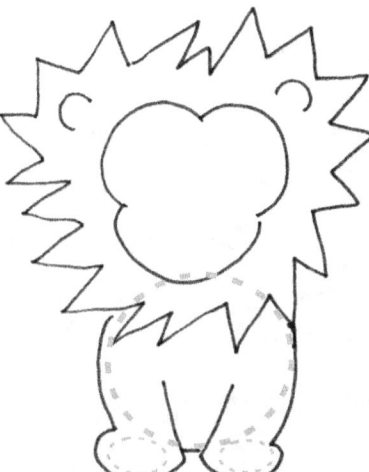

Imagine a circle and two ovals. Draw the body, legs and feet.

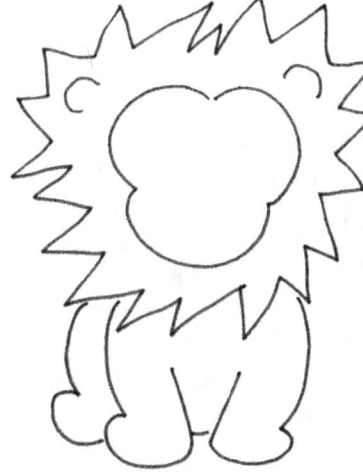

Follow the curve of the front leg and foot to create the back leg.

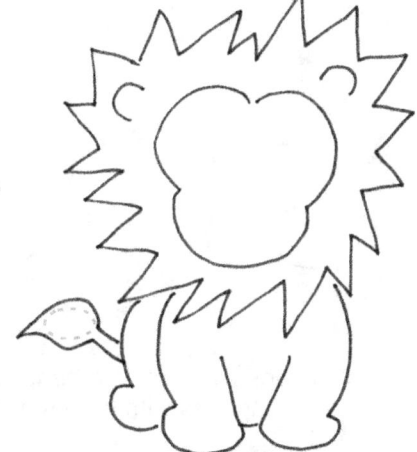

Imagine an oval and create a tail around it.

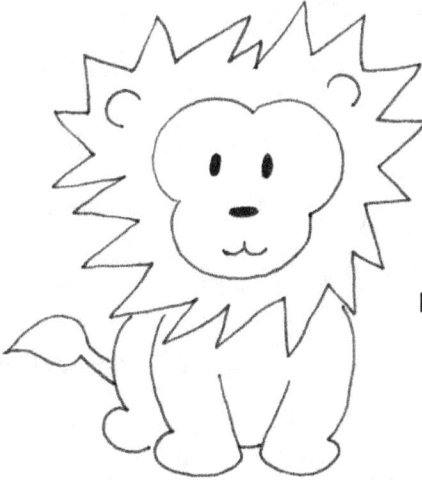

Finish by adding eyes and a nose.

How to Draw a Lizard

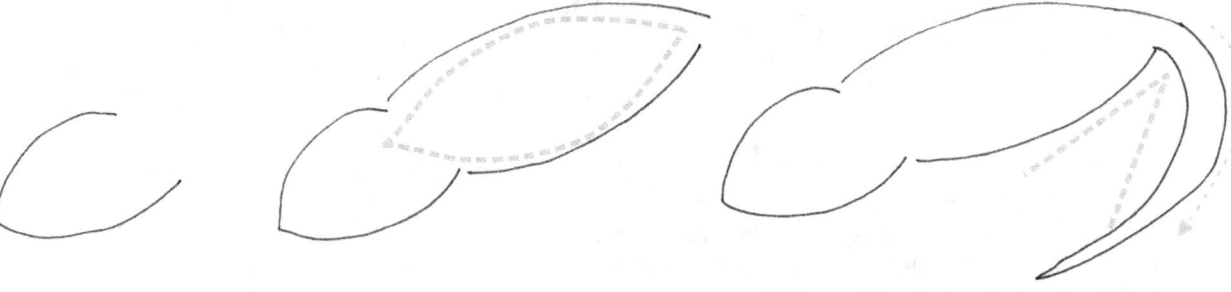

Draw a 'U'.   Add an open ended football shape.   Add a tail by the opening by drawing a curve, and look for the 'V' shape left between the body and tail.

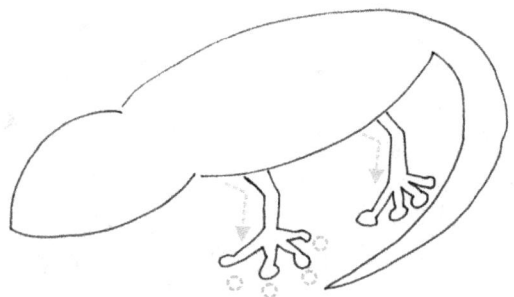

Draw legs by creating a bent line that flows into long toes with circles on the ends.

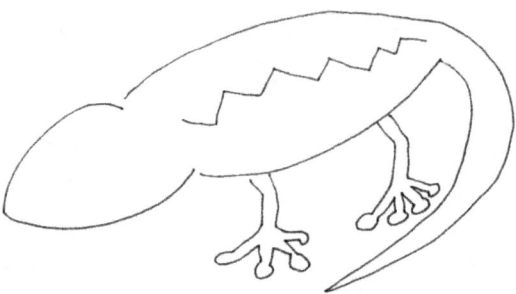

Draw a pointy zig zag line down the back.

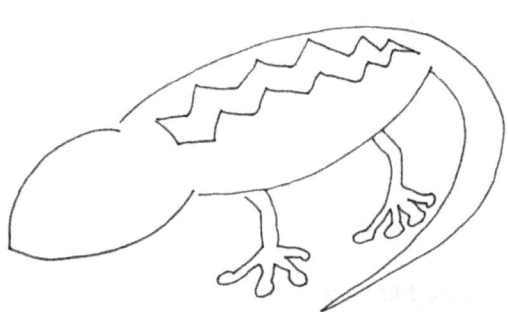

Match the line to create a thick stripe.

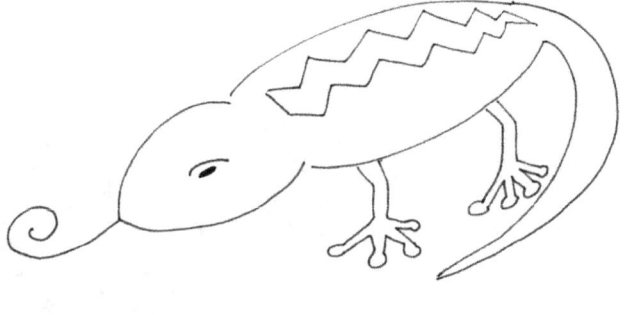

Add an eye and spiral tongue.

How to Draw a Monkey

Draw a football shape.

Cut football in half.

Imagine a circle and draw the top half on top of the football.

Add two half circles for ears.

Start under the chin and draw a long line for the arm and continue to create the leg. Imagine the rectangle between the arm and leg.

Draw the other side. Look for the square shape.

Imagine a circle and draw the tail curved around in a spiral.

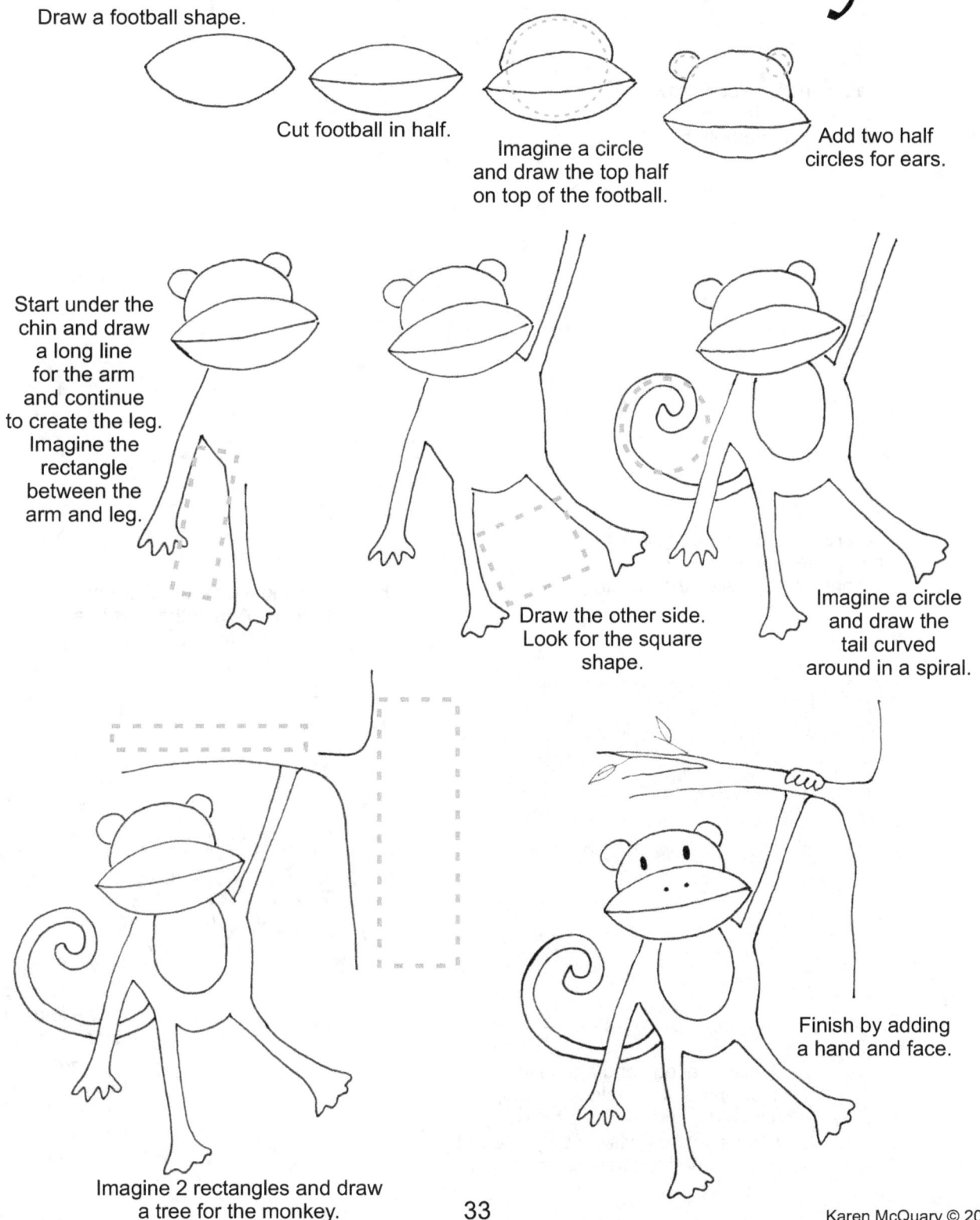

Imagine 2 rectangles and draw a tree for the monkey.

Finish by adding a hand and face.

33

How to Draw an Octopus

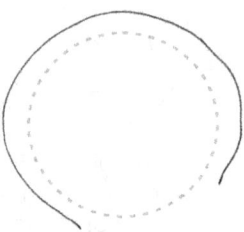

Imagine a circle and draw a partial circle with an opening at the bottom.

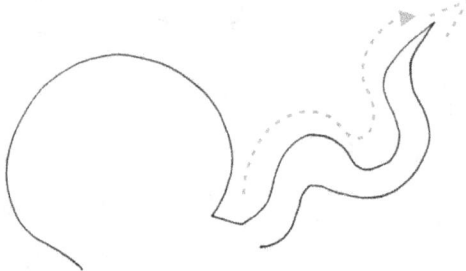

Starting at the opening, draw a curvy line that ends in a 'V' and a second line to match the first line.

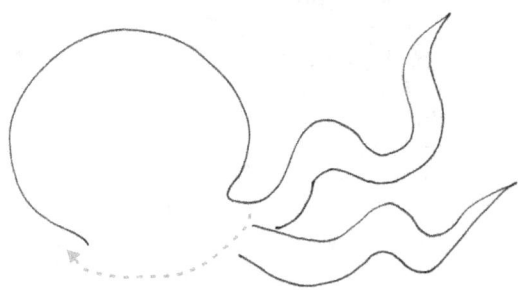

Keep drawing legs around the base of the circle. Attach the legs in a circular arc.

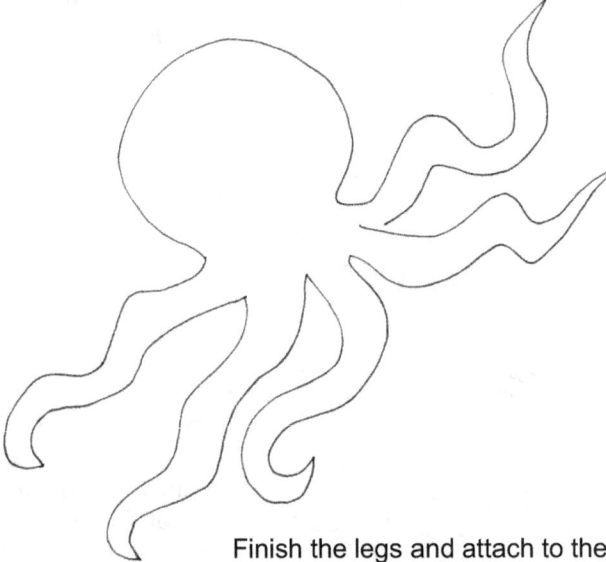

Finish the legs and attach to the other end of the circle. An octopus has 8 legs, but from one side only a few of its legs are visible so you don"t need to draw all 8.

Draw eyes and on a few legs draw a line on the inside of the leg to create the underside of the arm. Add suckers by making small circles.

34

How to Draw an Ostrich

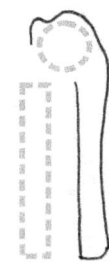
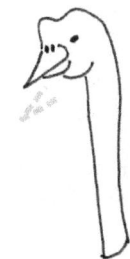

Imagine a small circle. Draw a 'bumpy' line around the circle. Continue into a long, skinny rectangle.

Add a 'V' shape to create the beak. Draw nostrils and an eye.

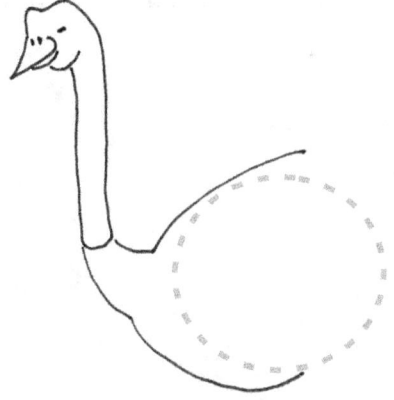
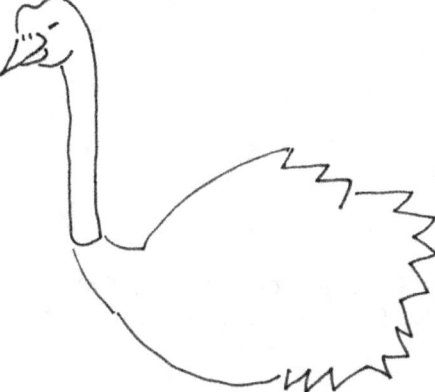

Imagine a large circle. Draw around it to create the body.

Draw several pointy shapes to create feathers.

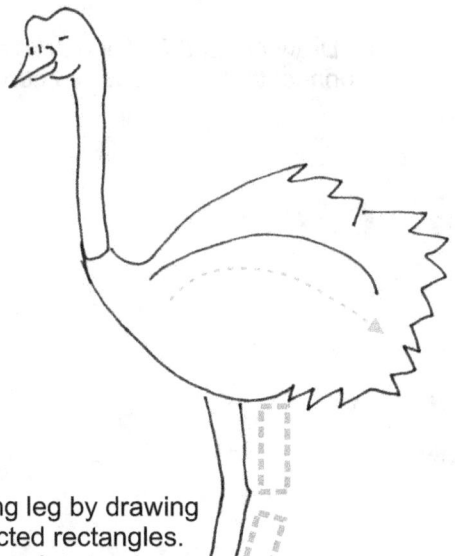
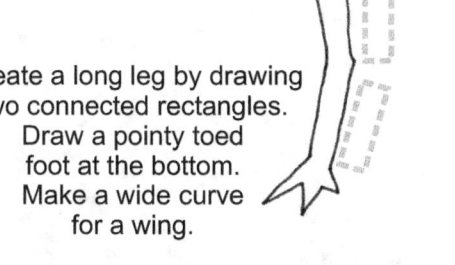
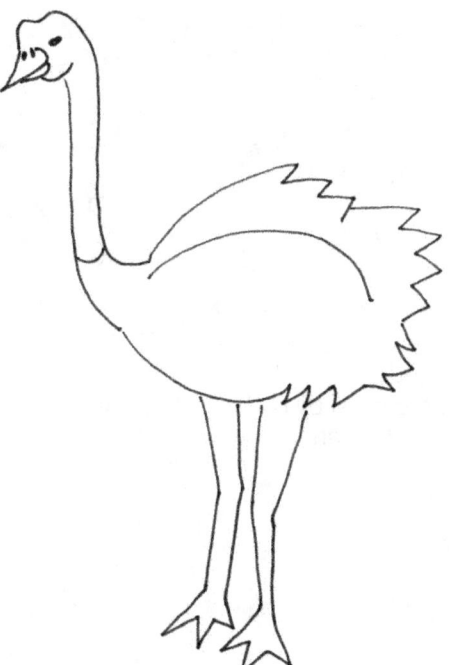

Create a long leg by drawing two connected rectangles. Draw a pointy toed foot at the bottom. Make a wide curve for a wing.

Draw a 2nd leg to match the first.

35

How to Draw an Otter

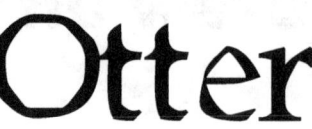

Imagine a rectangle and draw around it to create the head.

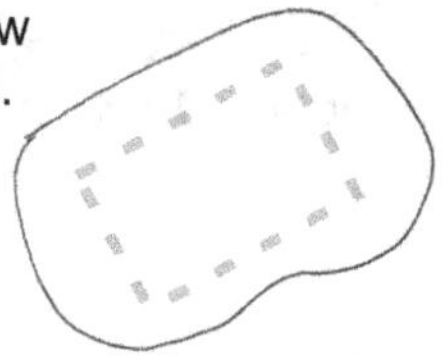

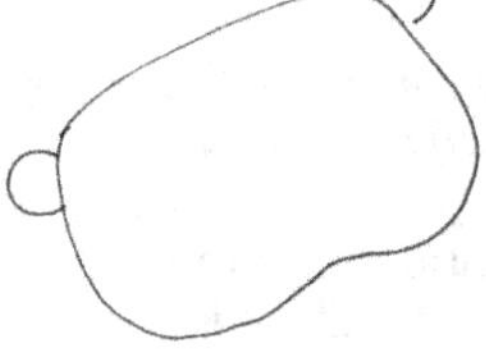

Add 2 'U' shapes to create ears on the side of the head.

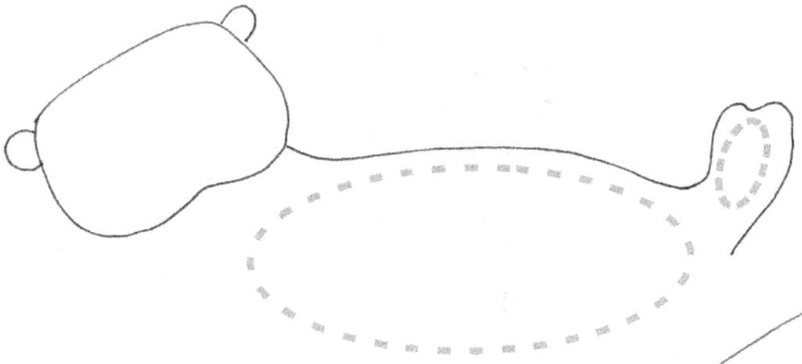

Imagine 2 oval shapes. Draw lines that create the stomach and foot.

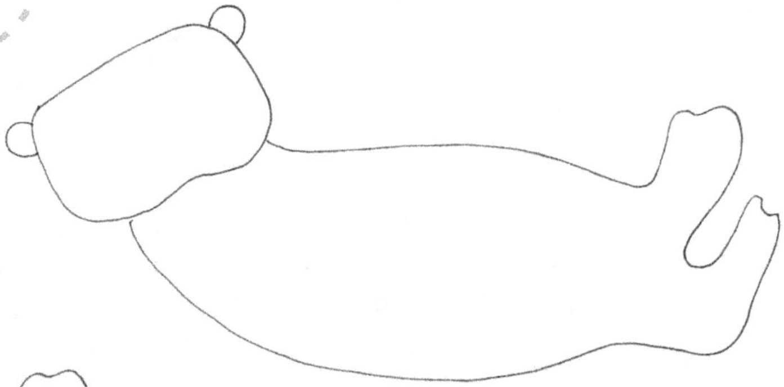

Draw the 2nd foot like the 1st and connect to the head with a curved line.

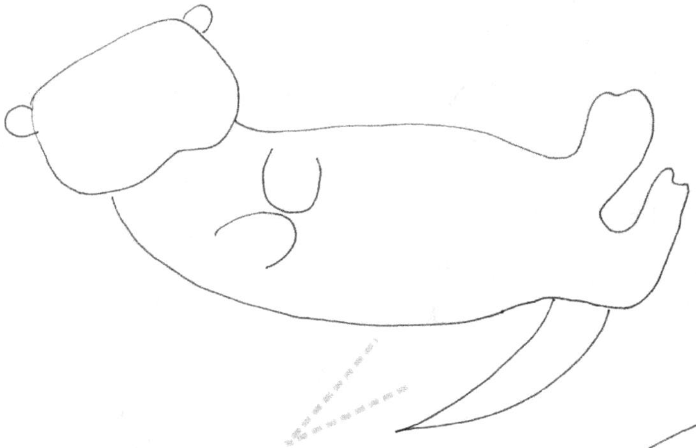

Create a tail by making a 'V' shape. Use 2 'U' shapes to make paws.

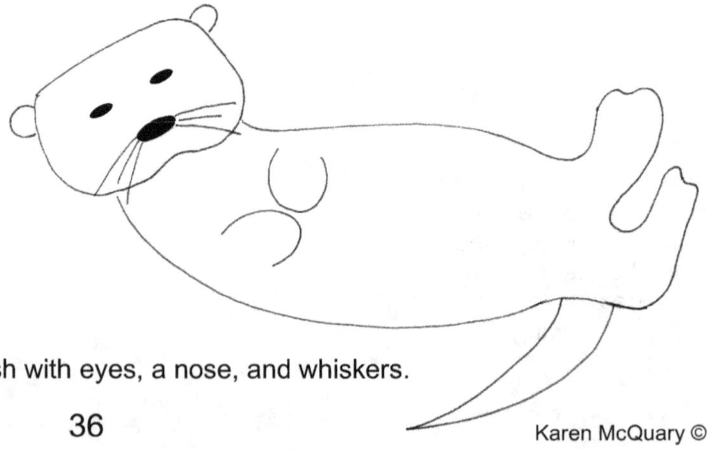

Finish with eyes, a nose, and whiskers.

Karen McQuary © 2010

How to Draw a Panda Bear

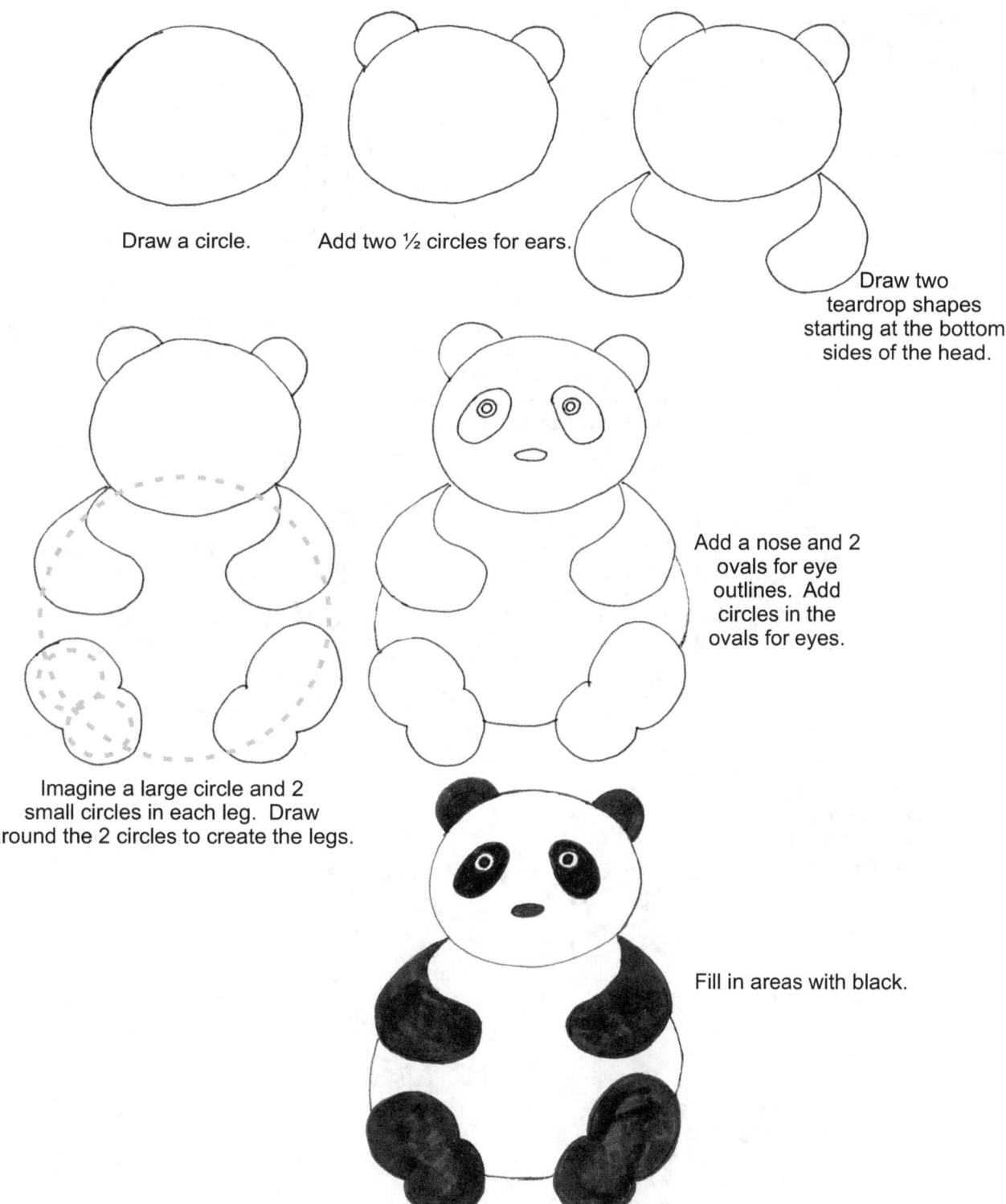

Draw a circle.

Add two ½ circles for ears.

Draw two teardrop shapes starting at the bottom sides of the head.

Imagine a large circle and 2 small circles in each leg. Draw around the 2 circles to create the legs.

Add a nose and 2 ovals for eye outlines. Add circles in the ovals for eyes.

Fill in areas with black.

How to Draw a

Peacock

Imagine a circle and draw around and up to create a body and beak.

Imagine a small circle and draw around it to finish the head and connect to the body. Add a half circle for a wing.

Draw lines from the body outward to create feathers.

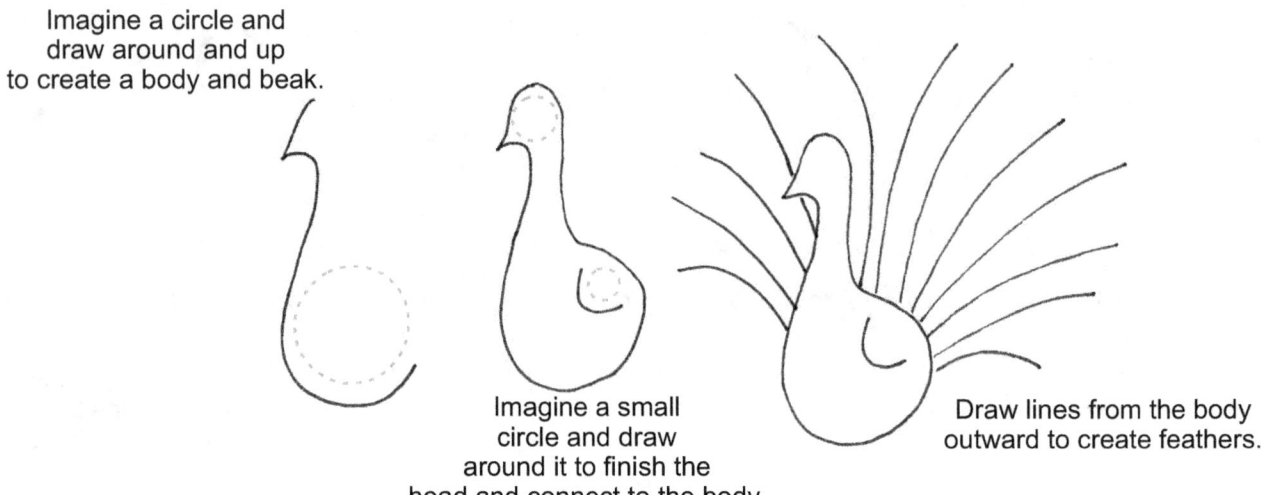

Create a 'V' shape at the end of each feather and draw a circle inside each 'V'.

Add extra lines to each feather base to create volume to the feathers.

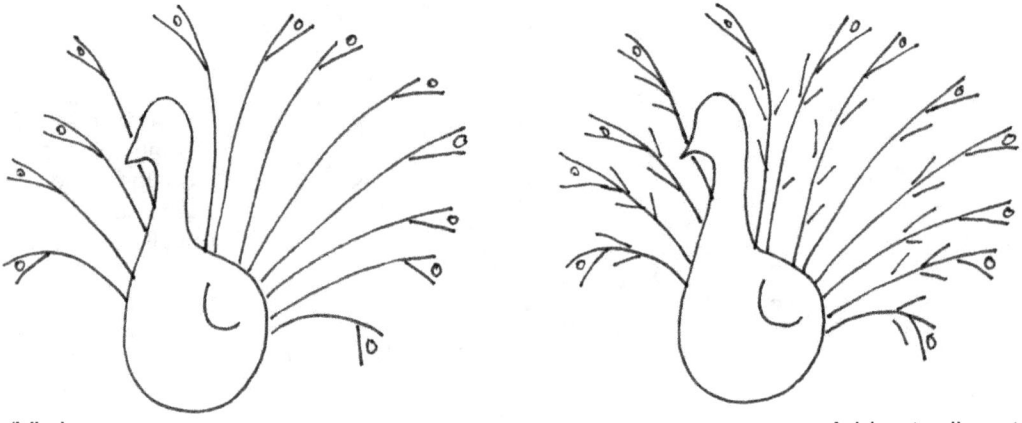

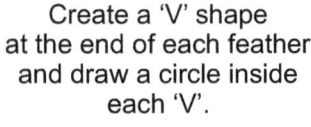

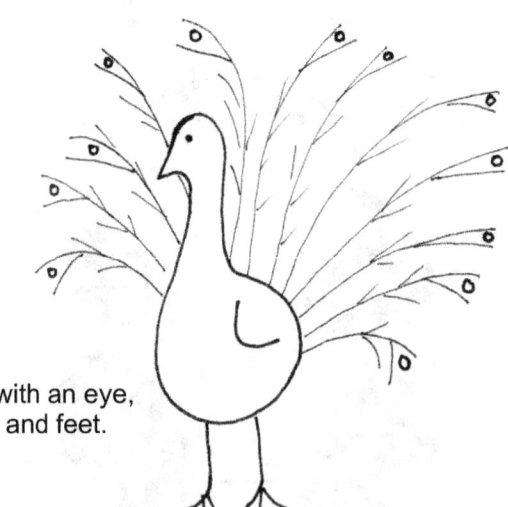

Finish with an eye, legs and feet.

38

How to Draw a Penguin

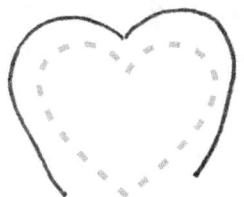

Imagine a heart shape and draw around it.

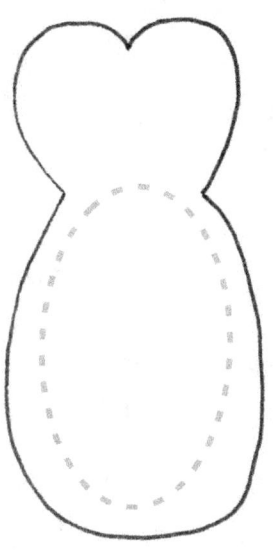

Imagine a long oval and draw around it, connecting to the top part.

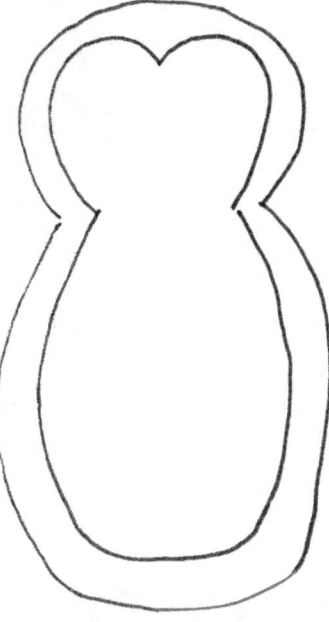

Follow the curve around and create a second outline.

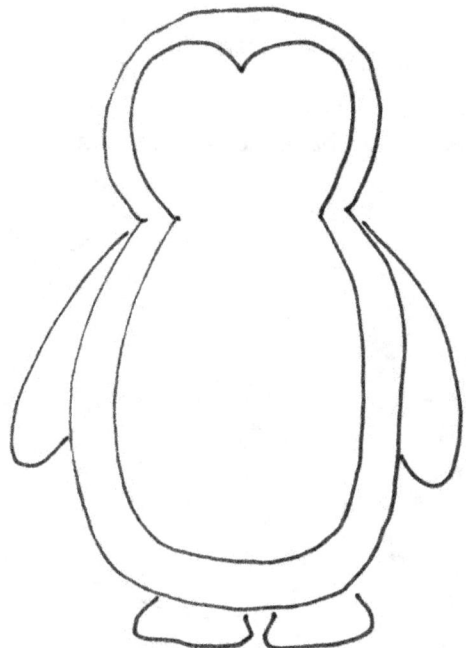

Add two wings and feet.

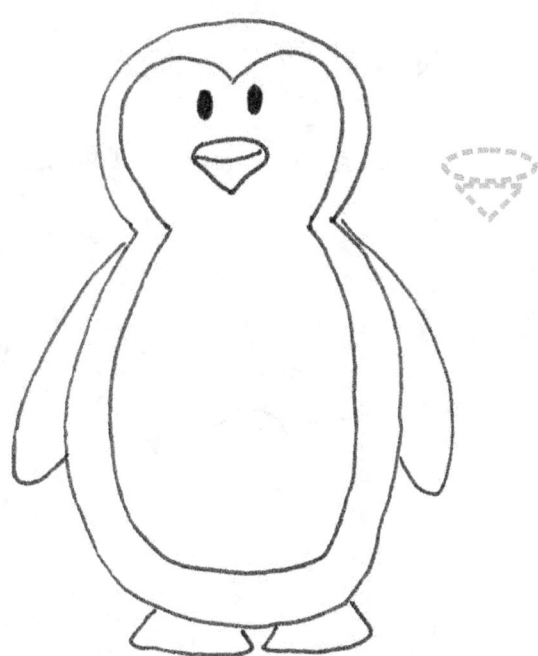

Finish with the eyes and beak. The beak is an oval with a triangle under it.

39

How to Draw a Polar Bear

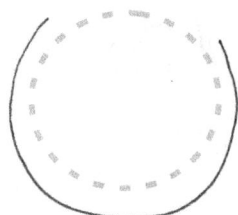

Draw a partial circle.

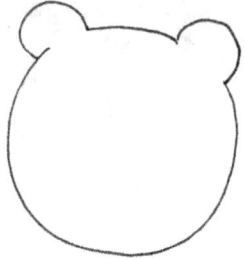

Add two ½ circles for ears and connect together.

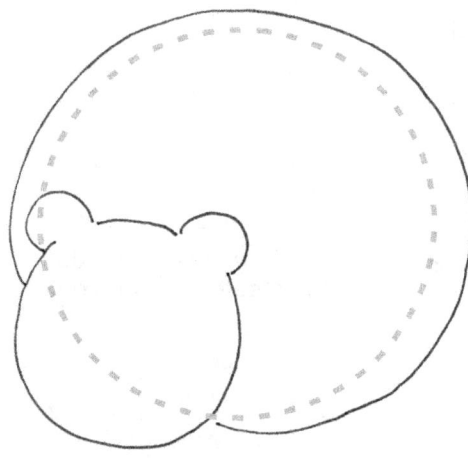

Draw a large circle behind the head.

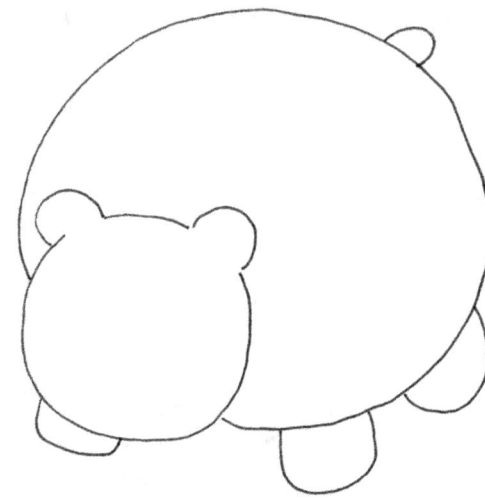

Add 4 'U' shapes to create feet and a tail.

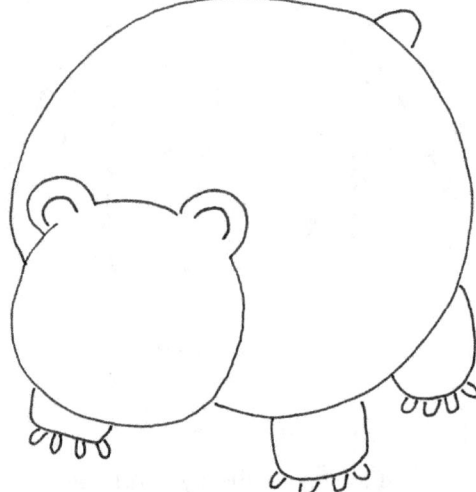

Add four 'U' shapes to each foot to make claws and small ½ circles in each ear.

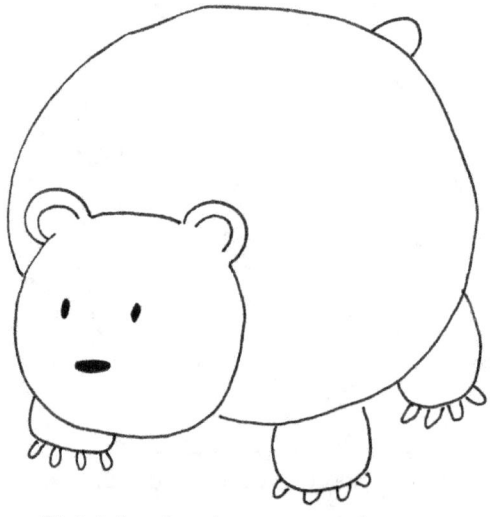

Finish by drawing eyes and a nose.

40

How to Draw a Porcupine

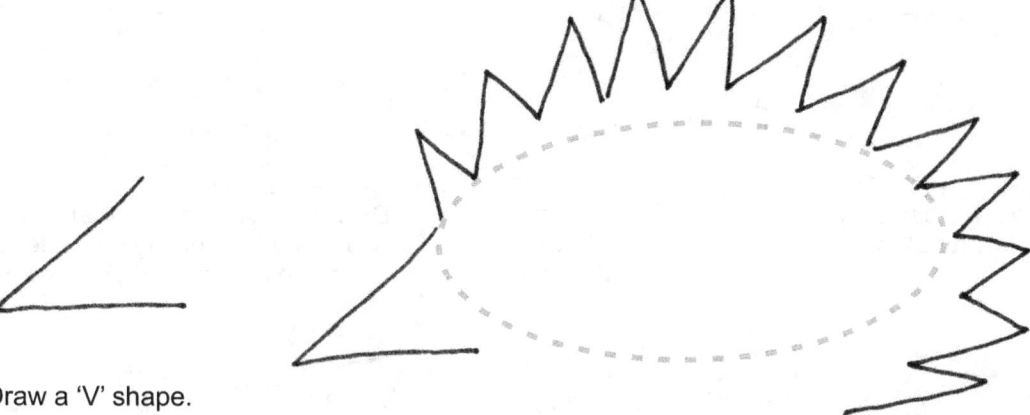

Draw a 'V' shape.

Imagine an oval and draw pointy 'V' shapes around the oval.

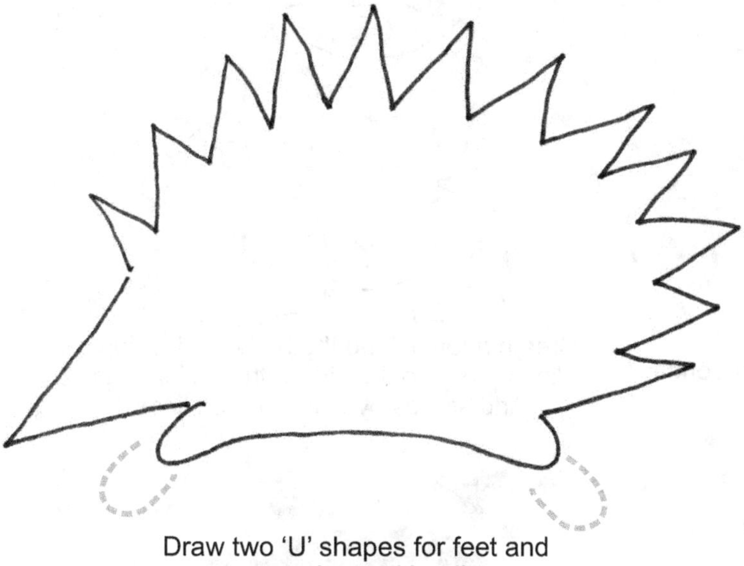

Draw two 'U' shapes for feet and connect them with a line.

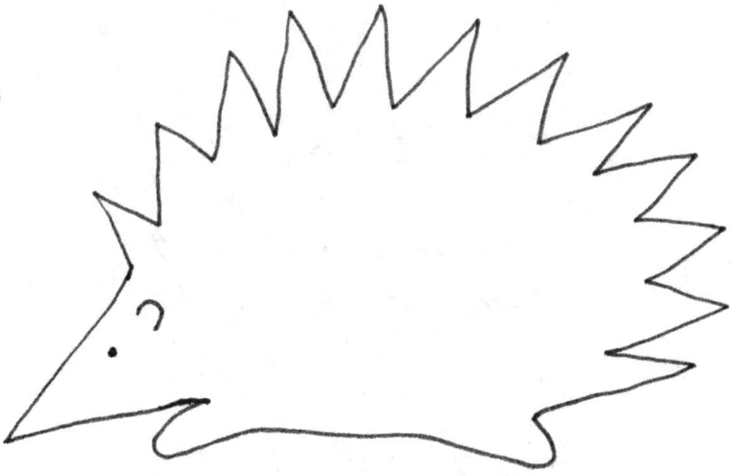

Finish with an eye and a 'U' shaped ear.

41

How to Draw a Raccoon

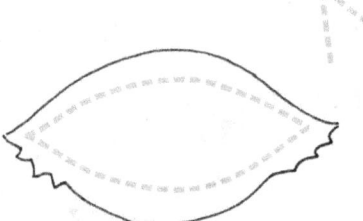

Draw a football shape with pointy fur at the ends.

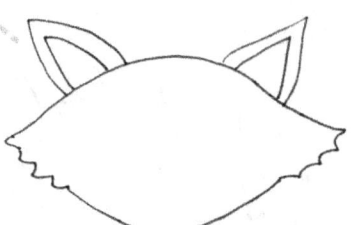

Create two ears by drawing 'V' shapes.

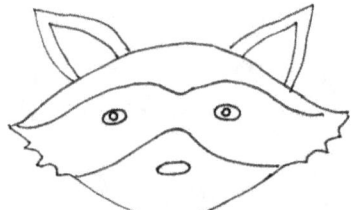

Draw the eyes and nose and create a stripe connecting one side to the other, around the eyes.

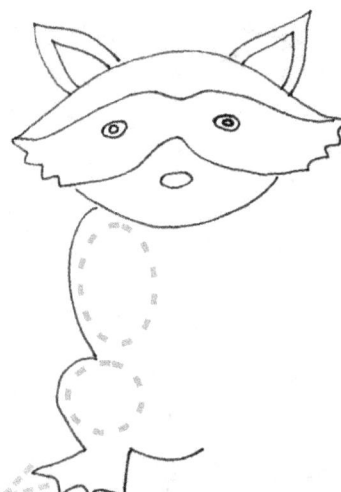

Imagine an oval and circle. Draw around them to create the side and leg. Add pointy toes.

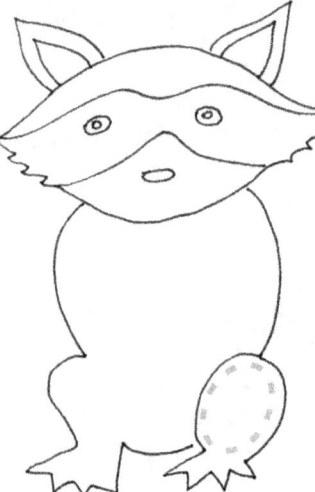

Draw the second leg.

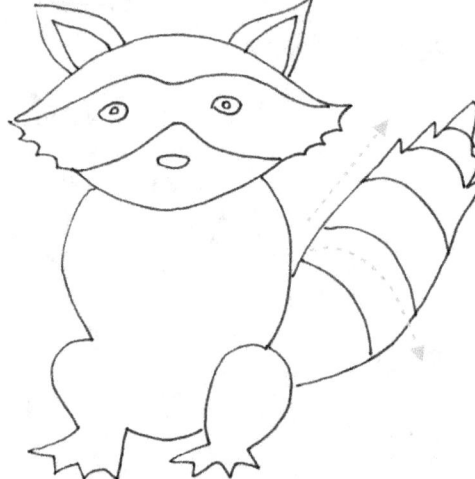

Create a tail behind the body by drawing a line up and to the side with a pointy end. Add stripes by using curved lines.

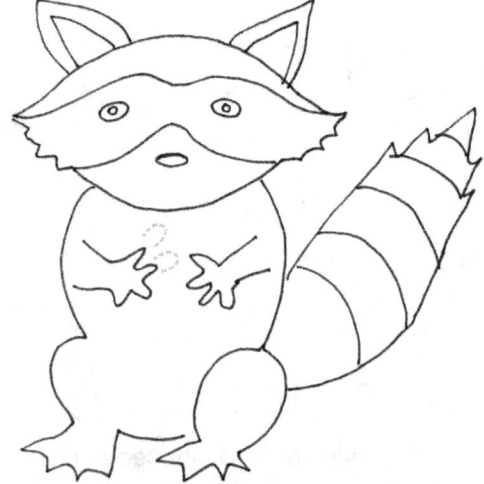

Add arms and hands. Fingers are made by drawing little 'U' shapes.

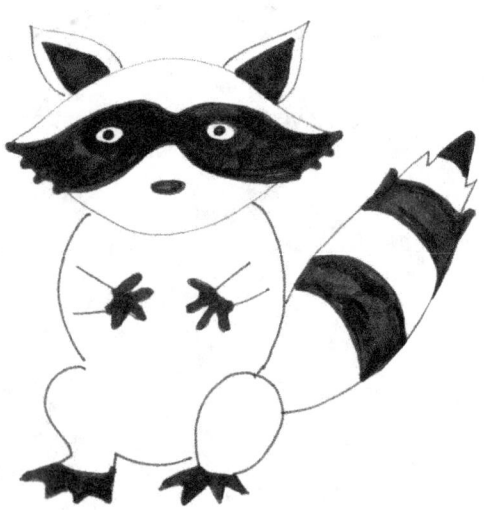

Fill in all dark sections.

42

Karen McQuary © 2010

How to Draw a
Rhinoceros

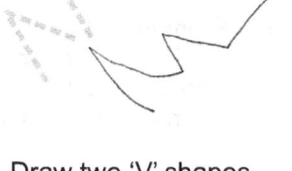

Draw two 'V' shapes.

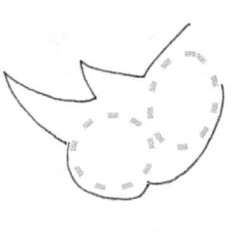

Imagine a circle and oval.
Draw around them to
create the head.

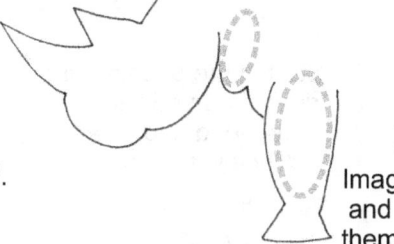

Imagine two ovals
and draw around
them to create the
neck and leg.

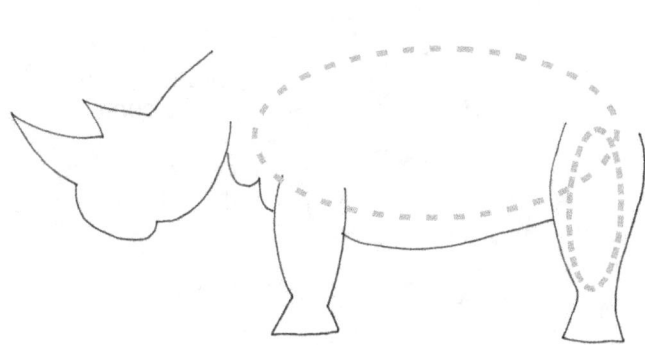

Imagine a large oval and draw
around it to create the body.
Draw the oval shaped back leg.

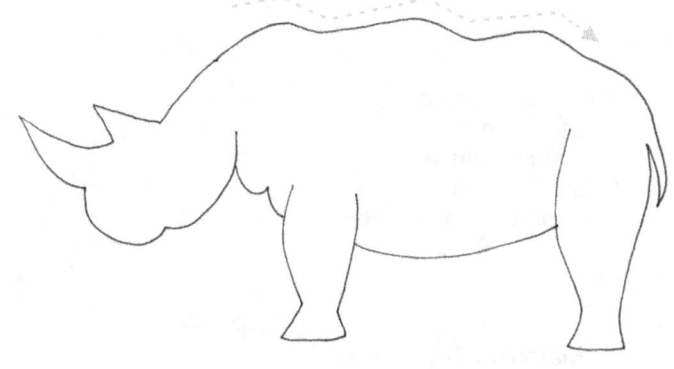

Start at the head and draw a bumpy line to
connect it to the tail.

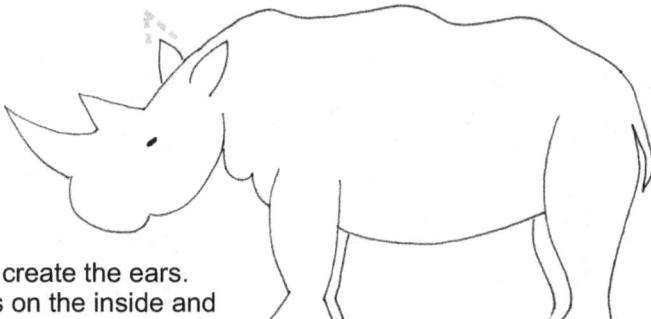

Use two 'V' shapes to create the ears.
Add a second set of legs on the inside and
draw an eye.

43

How to Draw a Snake

Imagine a heart shape and leave it open at the top.

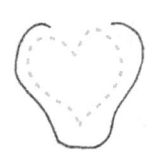

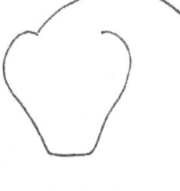

Start at the opening and draw a curved line over the head and down, below the body.

From the other side of the head, draw a matching line and connect to the first to make a 'V' shape.

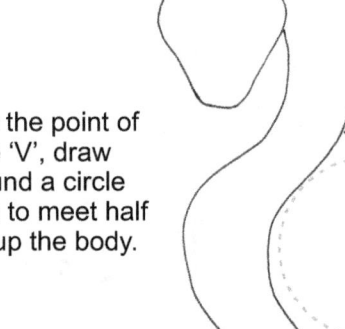

From the point of the 'V', draw around a circle shape to meet half way up the body.

Draw an oval in the center.

Matching the line of the body, extend it to the other side and curve down and back up to the body. The tail makes a 'V' point.

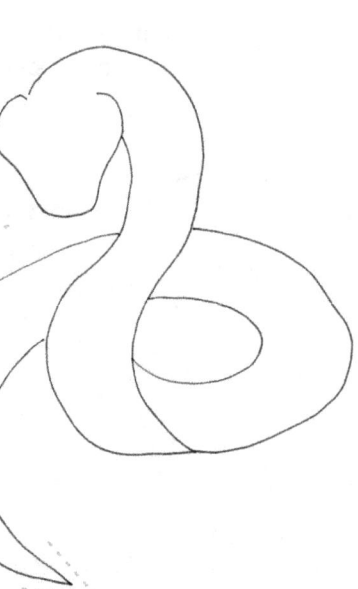

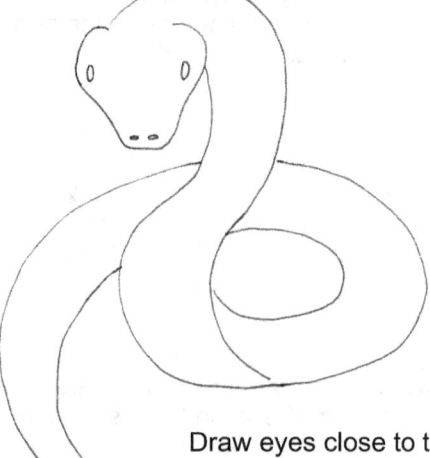

Draw eyes close to the side of the head and finish with the nose.

44

How to Draw a Squirrel

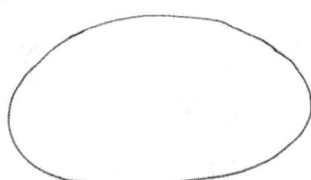

Draw an oval.

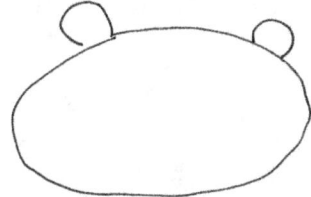

Add two 'U' shapes for ears.

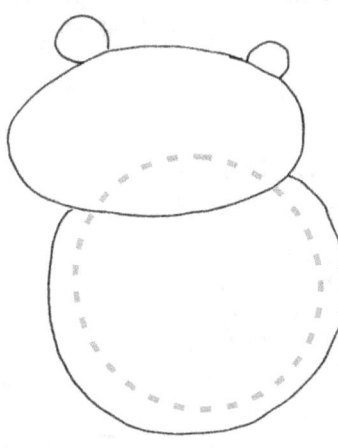

Imagine a large circle under the head.
Draw a partial circle around it.

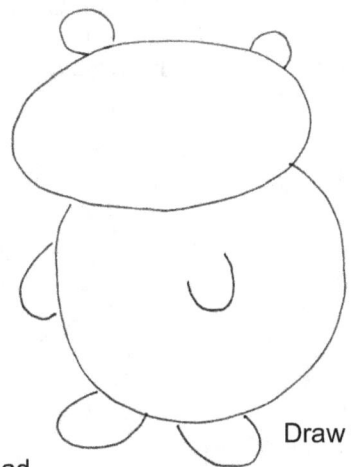

Draw four 'U' shapes to create
the feet and arms.

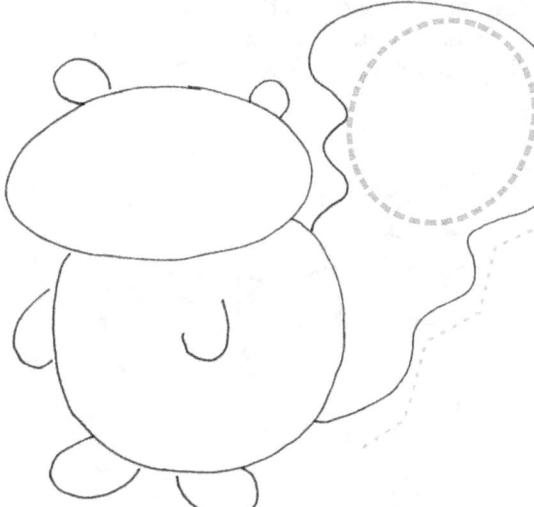

Imagine a circle shape behind the
body and create the tail by making a
bumpy curved line around it.

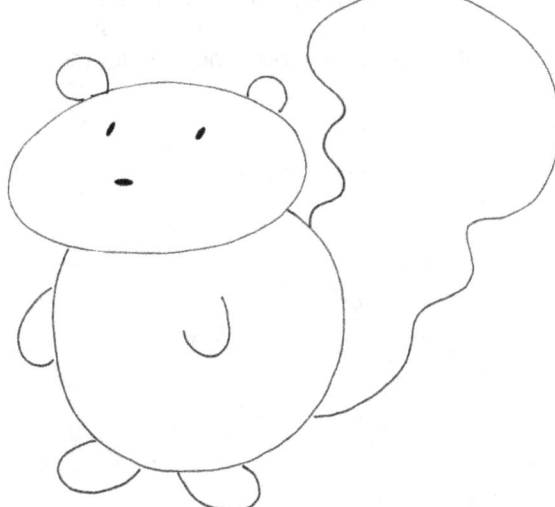

Finish with a face.

45

How to Draw a Tiger

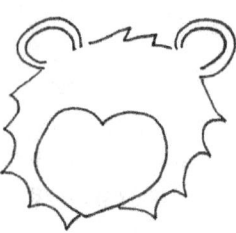

Draw a heart shape.

Imagine a circle around the heart. Create pointy fur around the heart. Leave the top open.

Create ears with 'U' shapes.

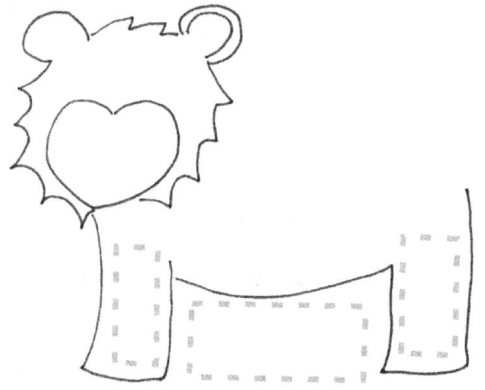

Start at the chin and imagine three rectangles. Draw around them to create legs and the stomach.

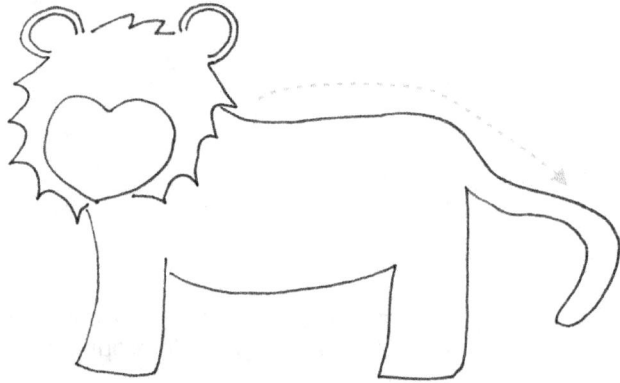

Start at the head and draw a curved line. Extend it out into a curved tail and connect back to the body.

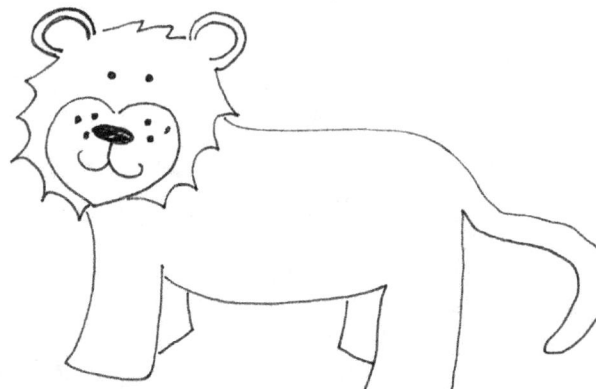

Draw the face and second set of legs on the inside.

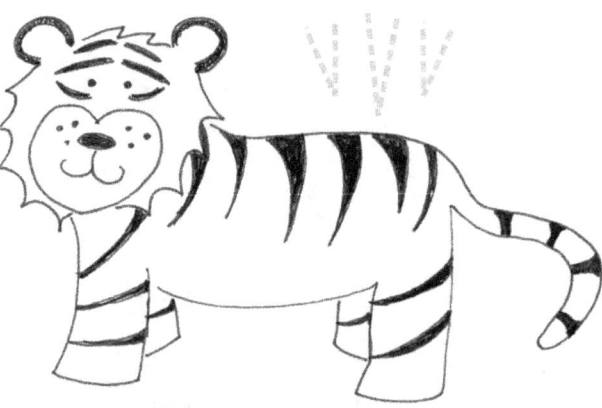

Add black stripes by drawing long, curved 'V' shapes and fill them in.

Karen McQuary © 2010

How to Draw a Turtle

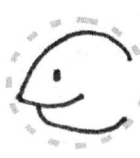

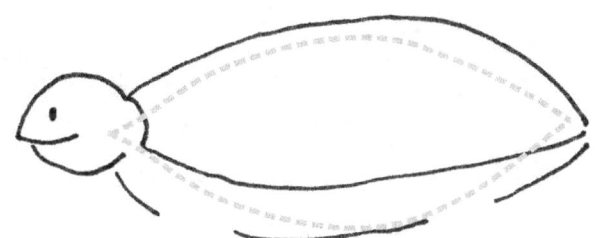

Imagine a circle.
Draw the face shape and eye.

Imagine a football shape. Draw it
next to the head and split it with a line.
Leave space for the legs and tail.

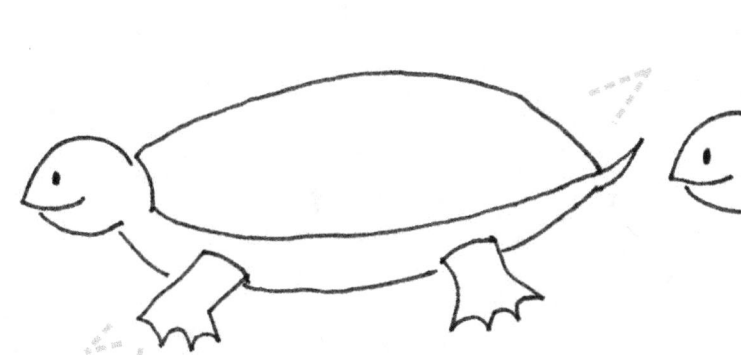

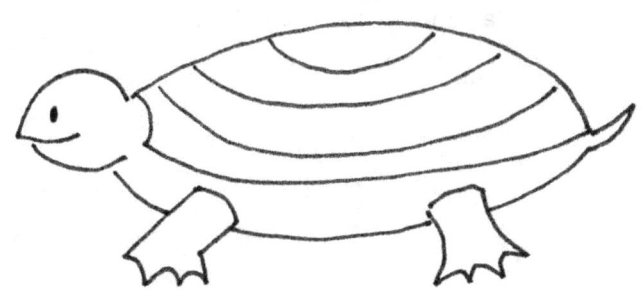

Add legs and feet with pointy toes and a
'V' shaped tail.

Draw stripes across the shell.

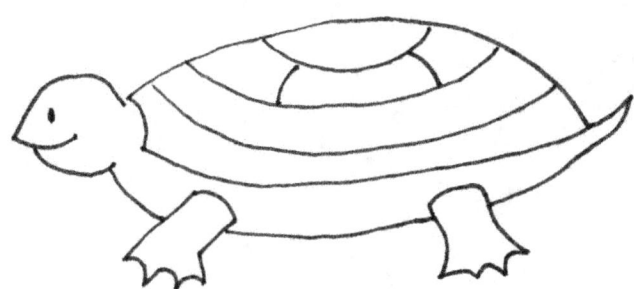

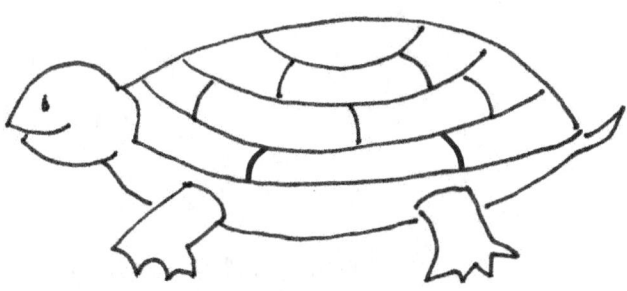

Draw two lines to cut one stripe into thirds.

Offset the next two stripes.

47

How to Draw a 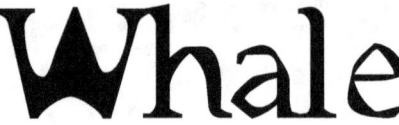 Whale

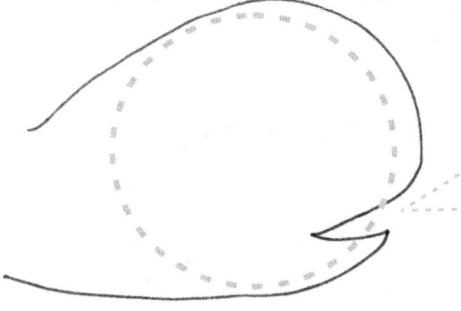

Imagine a circle with a 'V' shape cut out of it. Draw around it to create the head.

Continue drawing upward and create a tail from two 'V' shapes. The space between the body and the tail should be 'U' shaped. The tail should be taller than the whale's head.

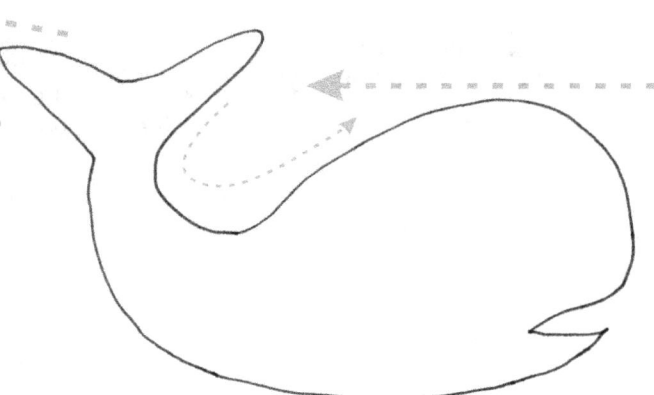

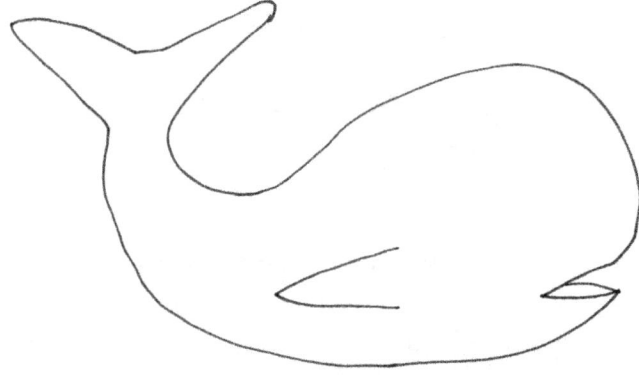

Add a 'V' shaped fin on the side of its body. Draw a small curved line in the mouth.

Finish by adding an eye, blowhole and a water burst.

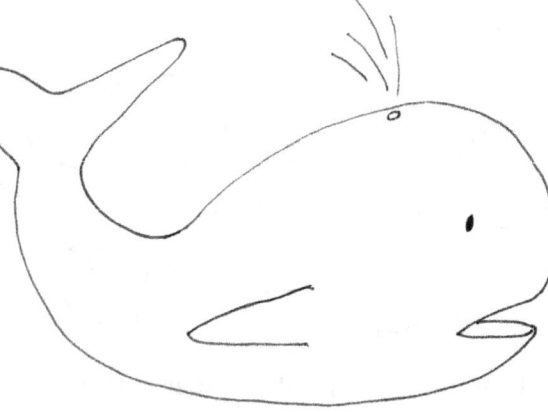